An Annotated Bibliography of Invalid Cookery Advice and Recipes in Australian Cookbooks 1860-1950

Peter Williams
BSc(Hons) DipNutrDiet MHP PhD FDAA

2018

Published by Willard Publishing, Canberra, Australia.

Printed in the United States by CreateSpace, Charleston SC

eStore address: www.CreateSpace.com/8447853

Copyright © by Peter Williams
The moral right of Peter Williams to be identified as the author of this work
has been asserted.

This work is licensed under the Creative Commons (CC) Attribution 3.0 Australia licence
To view a copy of the licence visit http://creativecommons.org/licences/by/3.0/

First published in 2018
Typeset in 12 point Garamond

 A catalogue record for this book is available from the National Library of Australia

ISBN 978-0-6483131-0-6 (paperback)
ISBN 978-0-6483131-1-3 (e-book)

Front cover illustration: Economic Cookery and Invalid Dishes (Bile Bean, 1903)
Rear cover illustration: Annotated Bibliography of Australian Domestic Cookery Books 1860s to 1950 (Hoyle, 2010)

TABLE OF CONTENTS

INTRODUCTION 5
    Background 5
    Method 5
    Standardisation of recipe names 7
    Summaries of Advice 7
    Arrangement of the entries 8
    Summary 10
    Thanks 11

CHRONOLOGICAL LIST 13
    Bibliography by Decades 13
        1860-1889 13
        1890-1899 21
        1900-1909 37
        1910-1919 53
        1920-1929 85
        1930-1939 113
        1940-1950 137

ALPHABETICAL TITLE LIST 157

REFERENCE LIST 167

ABOUT THE AUTHOR 181

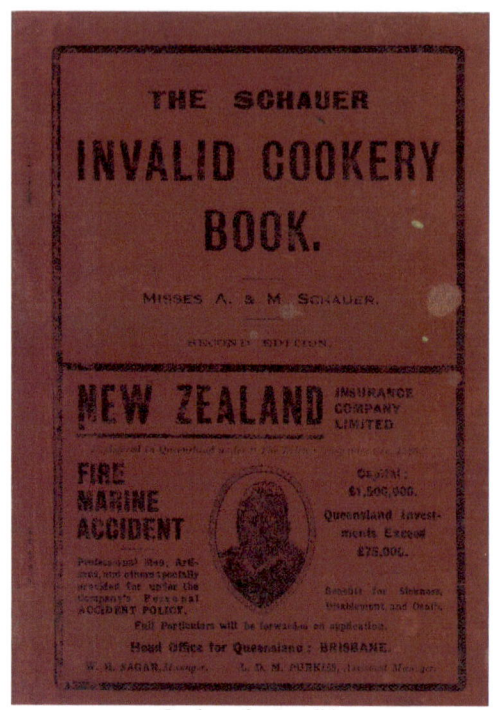

Cookery for Invalids
(A Schauer & Schauer, 1912)

Notes and Recipes on Invalid Cookery and Nutrition
(Giles & Rapley, 194-?)

Adelect Invalid and Convalescent Cookery
(Benson, 1942)

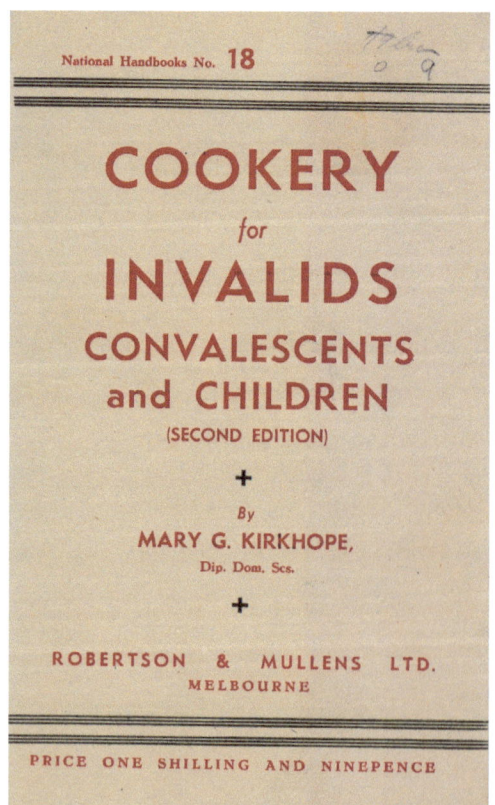

Cookery for Invalids, Convalescents and Children
(Kirkhope, 1944)

INTRODUCTION

This bibliography documents the invalid cookery entries in early Australian cookbooks, and summarises the types of recipes and dietary advice for such cookery that were included in the books.

Background

My interest in this topic arose from my work as a dietitian managing clinical dietetic and foodservice departments at Royal Prince Alfred Hospital in Sydney in the late 1970s, where my duties included menu planning. One element of this work involved understanding how best to meet the food requirements of patients recovering from illness or surgery – a subject that often seemed to be based more on art and experience than any solid scientific foundation. This interest led me to undertake research on the food preferences of hospital inpatients, culminating in my PhD research, published in 1994, on *Food in Hospitals – a study of the menus and food service systems in New South Wales hospitals*.

I began collecting old Australian cookbooks in 1986 and by the time of my retirement in 2012 I had collected 332 titles published up until 1950. The Australian market for books in the nineteenth century was small, and British publishers continued to supply the standard British works to the Australian market. However, from the 1860s onwards a growing number of local cookbooks were published. These books often included dedicated sections of recipes aimed at guiding those responsible for preparing food for invalids or convalescents. Various terms were used to describe these recipes including foods for invalids, convalescents, or the sickroom. For simplicity in this publication, the umbrella term "invalid cookery" is used.

Method

There are two main bibliographies of Australian cookbooks. A publication of cookbooks published prior to 1941 was produced by the Emily McPherson branch of the RMIT libraries in Melbourne, with 576 entries (Austin, 1987). A much larger, authoritative reference work by John Hoyle catalogues Australian domestic cookery books from the 1860s to 1950; most of the books referenced by Hoyle are held in Australian public libraries (Hoyle, 2010). His publication has 1418 entries, but that number includes separate bibliographic entries for multiple editions of the same title; the total number of unique titles is 719. However, as both Austin and Hoyle note, these two bibliographies are incomplete. More than a hundred of the cookbooks in my private collection are not included in either Austin or Hoyle and still further titles are likely to be discovered.

To prepare this bibliography, all books listed in the two published bibliographies were examined, along with the additional items in the author's private collection, and 42 other cooking or recipe books in the collections of the National Library of Australia and the State Library of NSW that were not captured in either of the published bibliographies. The location of items was identified by a search in the Trove database (https://trove.nla.gov.au). Most of the publications are cookbooks, but in some cases they are more general books on health, home maintenance, or use of new kitchen appliances, which also included a selection of recipes. This bibliography lists recipes that are contained in a separate section called invalid, convalescent or sickroom cookery. If books did not include such a specially indicated section, any recipes that had a word in the title that indicated their intended use (e.g. Invalid's soup) are also noted.

Many of the earlier cookbooks also include general advice or rules about how to feed a sick person. This advice ranges from the safe preparation of the food itself to the arrangement and service of a meal tray, and ways to tempt a patient with poor appetite. The text of these entries is also noted, but as much of this information was common across many titles, only representative samples are reproduced in this bibliography.

The publication time frame for the books examined is from 1860 to 1950, for two reasons. The first is that this corresponds with the dates in Hoyle's bibliography. Secondly, the number of recipe books published grew rapidly after the Second World War and most of these newer books no longer included advice about invalid cookery.

One particular bibliographic problem I encountered was determining the date of publication of many early books. Hoyle notes that in his bibliography only 37% of the books included a date from the publisher or printer. Where possible he provided estimates of dates using information such as handwritten annotations, library acquisition dates, and internal evidence from advertisements, calendars and telephone numbers. Where books had no publication date, I have used the estimates of Hoyle, or those in the Trove catalogue entries, for this bibliography.

Standardisation of recipe names

Inevitably, the sources often use different formatting/spelling for the same recipe term. E.g. beef tea/beef-tea; egg nog/eggnog/egg-nog/egg nogg; black currant/blackcurrant; omelet/omelette; blanc-mange/blancmange/blanc manger; soufflé/soufflés/soufflée; scallop/scalloped/scollop/scalloped; calf's foot/calves' feet/calf foot/calves' foot; and home-made/home made/homemade. For simplicity, in this bibliography the spelling of these and other names has been standardised on the term preferred in the *Macquarie Dictionary* and applied throughout. This should enable researchers to search on one form of a recipe name, rather than trying to think of all the variants it might appear under. In the original texts there is also a variety of spelling of words such as peptonized/peptonised and albumenized/albumenised. I have standardised these spellings to the "–ised" format.

Summaries of Advice

The text in the Advice sections is generally quoted verbatim from the originals, which means that some of the odd phrasing and unusual spelling is retained unchanged. Where the author has provided numbered rules, these are given in the summaries. In other cases, general paragraphed text is used, although this only reproduces the parts of the material particularly related to menus or cooking. If the advice is very similar to that in other cookbooks, I have not always reproduced the text but an entry note in square brackets indicates the presence of some general advice on invalid cookery. I have mostly omitted other more general nursing advice.

Arrangement of the entries

This bibliography is presented in three sections:

<u>1. Chronological List</u>

The main detailed entries are provided chronologically using the date of the earliest available edition; the entries are grouped by decade of publication. Where more than one title was published in the same year, the entries under that date are arranged alphabetically by title. Each entry lists the publication date, book title (and edition information where relevant), and an author-date citation linking to the book's full publication details in the Reference List in Section 3. In addition, a note in square brackets indicates either the bibliographic number in the Hoyle bibliography, or the information that the book is 'Not in Hoyle' (for those items published up to 1950).

Two sets of information are summarised for each entry:

<u>Advice</u> (which includes suggestions and rules for food preparation and feeding of invalids) and

<u>Recipes</u> (which lists all the recipes defined as suitable for invalids or convalescents).
Recipes are listed in the order they appear in the cookbook. The source publication page numbers for this information is also noted. Where recipes were not co-located in sections, the relevant recipe pages are listed immediately after each individual recipe in the chronological list.

As many editions as possible of each title were searched and reviewed, and later editions are listed under the first entry, noting any changes in content over time. For example, the contents of 14 editions of the *Goulburn Cookery Book* – published from 1899 to 1975 – are summarised below the entry for the first edition in 1899.

Examples of some book covers or title pages are provided as illustrations at the beginning of each decade of the chronological list.

2. Alphabetical Title List

The second section is an alphabetical list of titles with the reference citation added in a separate column. For simplicity of searching, only short versions of titles are used and the word "The" at the beginning of titles is omitted.

3. Reference List

The third section provides details of the authors and publication details, using the APA referencing style. Entries are arranged alphabetically by author. For multi-edition books, reference citations have only been included when an edition has some changed content about invalid cookery. For example, of the 15 editions of the *Commonsense Cookery Book* published from 1914 to 2013, only five included changed content. Citations are given for those five editions in the Chronological List and included as separate entries in the Reference List.

Here is an example of how one book appears in the three lists:

1. Chronological List

1924

South Australian Presbyterian Cookery Book.
(Chalmers Church Friendship Club, 1924) [Hoyle 1090]
Advice (p59)
Don't walk in a sick room, glide and wear rubbers on heels; close doors quietly and speak quietly. Do not leave food in a patient's room or on kitchen table for flies to crawl over; put food away or use a net or butter cloth over same.
Recipes (pp59-60)
- Salsify and oyster plant soup
- Artichoke soup
- Large bean soup
- Lentil
- Boiled onions

2. Alphabetical Title List

South Australian Presbyterian Cookery Book.	(Chalmers Church Friendship Club, 1924)

3. Reference List

Chalmers Church Friendship Club. (1924). *South Australian Presbyterian Cookery Book*. Adelaide: Gillingham Swan & Co Ltd.

Summary

The total number of unique titles collected in this bibliography (ignoring the multiple editions of any one title) is summarised in the table below.

Date of first publication	Number of books	Percentage
1860-1889	10	4
1890-1899	22	10
1900-1909	26	11
1910-1919	42	19
1920-1929	51	23
1930-1939	40	18
1940-1950	33	15
Total	224	100

Overall, the 224 books include recipes for 1471 different dishes. By far the most common recipes are for beef tea, barley water, gruel and meat broths, with over 100 recipes for each. Recipes for beverages, desserts and soups make up nearly 60% of all entries and there are very few at all for vegetables, sandwiches, salads or sauces. Offal recipes are common and many are for raw liver dishes. Until the late 1940s, when vitamin B12 was synthesised, a diet including raw liver was the main mode of treatment for pernicious anaemia (Minot & Murphy, 1926; P. Muskett, 1908).

There is no particularly noticeable change in the recipes over time, suggesting perhaps that many authors continued to copy older references on the topic rather than presenting new information.

Similarly, the advice on feeding invalids is often identical in various texts and focuses primarily on the service of small dainty serves, avoidance of fat and heavy seasoning, and not bothering the patient with choices about the food they are to receive. The rules given in 1905 in *Principles of Practical Cookery for School Pupils* are much the same as the advice forty years later in the *Victorian Country Women's Recipe Book 1945-1946*.

I hope that this publication will encourage others to undertake further dietetic and culinary research on this fascinating topic.

Thanks

I first have to acknowledge the splendid work of John Hoyle in developing his bibliography of Australian Cookery Books; without that publication this companion volume would not have been produced. The wonderful support of my long-suffering husband Geoffrey Ballard, who put up with my many days spent in libraries and in front of the computer, was essential to allow me to complete this work. The meticulous editorial advice of Tessa Wooldridge has greatly improved this book as a whole, but any remaining errors are mine alone. I would like to dedicate this work to the memory of Jo Rogers who, as Chief Dietitian at Royal Prince Alfred Hospital, first employed me as a dietitian and introduced me to the world of hospital foodservice and the challenges of feeding sick patients.

Peter Williams

May 2018

CHRONOLOGICAL LIST
Bibliography by Decades

1860-1889

Cookery Recipes for the People (Pearson, 1889)

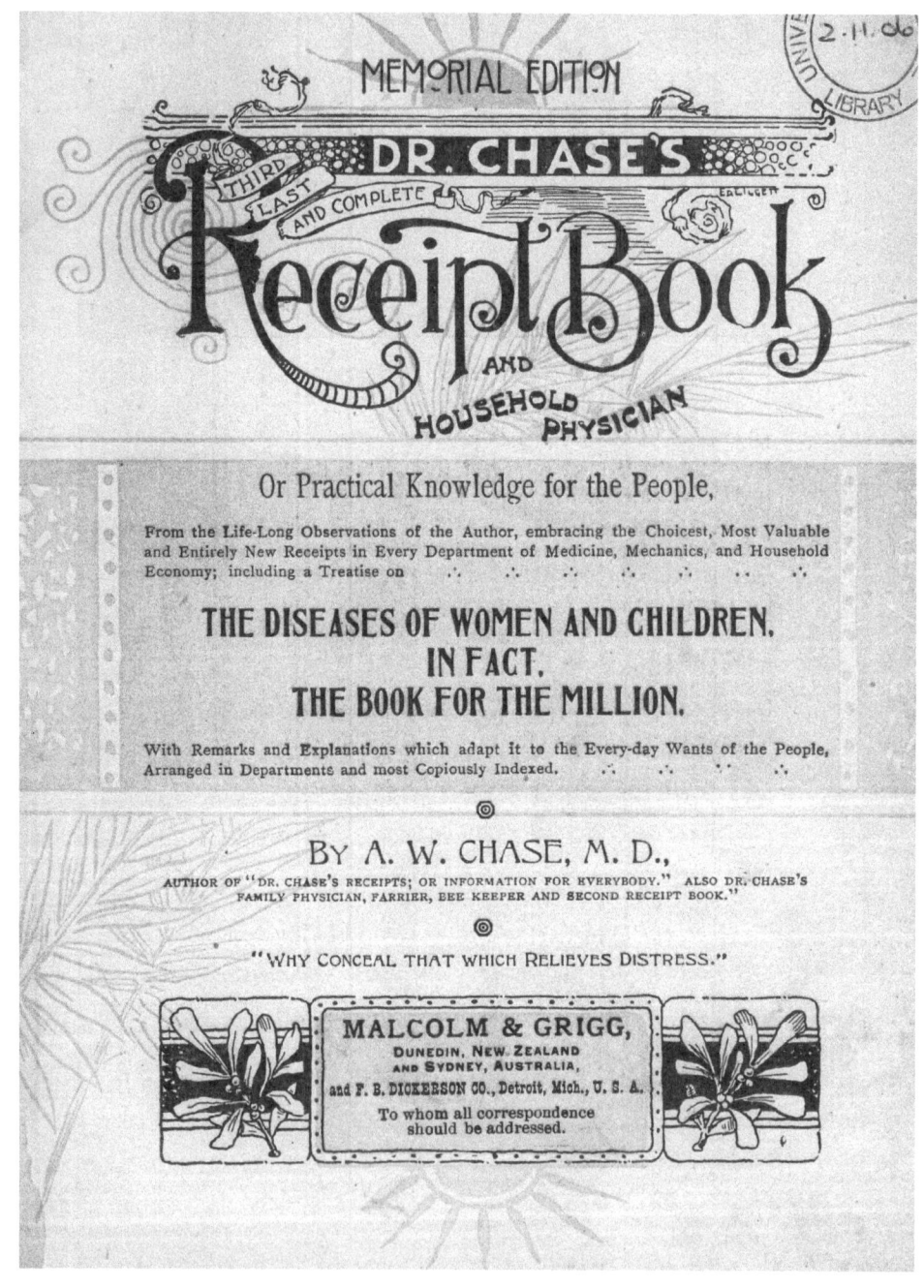

Dr Chase's Third Last and Complete Receipt Book and Household Physician (Chase, 1887)

1864

The English and Australian Cookery Book: Cookery for the many, as well as for the upper ten thousand/by an Australian aristologist. (Abbott, 1864) [Hoyle 5]

Recipe (p158)

- Invalid biscuits [butter, milk, sugar, yeast and caraway seeds]

1877

The Australian Cook. A complete manual of cookery suitable for the Australian colonies (2nd edition). (Wilkinson, 1877) [Hoyle 1374]

Recipes (pp9; 114-115)

- Beef tea
- Chicken broth
- Dr Wratislaw's beef tea
- Barley water
- Bread and milk
- Toast water
- Lemonade

1882

Australian Plain Cookery (2nd edition). (A Practical Cook, 1882) [Hoyle 91]

Recipes (pp122-124)

- Barley water
- Cream of barley
- Barley gruel
- Beef tea (2 recipes)
- Raw beef tea
- Sago gruel
- Oatmeal gruel
- Oatmeal jelly
- Arrowroot
- Water arrowroot
- Rice water
- Apple water
- Strengthening drink for an invalid [eggs, sugar, sherry and soda water]
- Suet and milk
- Milk and rum
- Fish for invalids
- Invalid's soup
- Invalid's pudding
- Arrowroot pudding
- Egg wine

1884

The Cook's Guide and Housekeeper's and Butler's Assistant. (Francatelli, 1884) [Hoyle 551]

Recipes (pp445-449; 452-454)

- Hop tea
- Linseed tea
- Lime-flower tea
- Marshmallow water
- Violet tea
- Infusion of roses
- Chamomile tea
- Iceland moss jelly
- Hyssop tea
- Saffron tea
- Orange flower tea
- Mulberry water
- Dandelion tea

- Refreshing drink for sore throat [infusion of barberries, violets and honey]
- How to make tea
- How to make coffee
- Gruel
- Caudle
- A pudding for infants
- Infants' food
- Scotch pudding
- Barley water
- Savoury custard

1886

A Course of Four Lectures on Sick Nursing. (Hamilton, 1886) [Not in Hoyle]

Recipes (pp17-23)
- Boiled egg
- Poached egg
- Egg drinks (with milk, wine, brandy, tea or coffee)
- Milk and soda water (or lime water)
- Barley gruel
- Toast water
- Beef tea
- Boiled fish
- Fried fish
- Oatmeal gruel

1887

Dr Chase's Third Last and Complete Receipt Book and Household Physician.
(Originally published in Chicago; this edition Dunedin and Sydney) **(Chase, 1887)**
[Hoyle 219]

Advice (p304)

While the patient's condition will allow them to use plain and substantial food, and the usual drink, as tea and coffee, not too strong, it is best that they have them; but with the weak and debilitated the delicacies must take their place; and I desire to call especial attention to, and to give my sanction and advice, that if any special thing is craved, be it food or drink, I would most positively allow it, in moderation.

Both food and drink should be given regularly in reasonable quantities.

Recipes (pp304-317)
- Beef tea (4 recipes)
- Oyster essence
- Chicken broth
- Mutton broth
- Beef broth
- Veal broth
- Vegetable broth
- Milk porridge with raisins
- Oatmeal porridge, or gruel
- Cornmeal gruel, or porridge
- Brown cornmeal gruel, or cakes, for warm stomachs
- Milk and rice gruel
- Tamarind whey, cooling and laxative
- Tamarind water, for fever patients
- Wine whey
- Sour milk whey
- Chicken water
- Barley water
- Chicken panada

- Plain panada (2 recipes)
- Corn coffee, for the sick, or for a nauseous stomach
- Corn tea
- Rice coffee, especially nice for children or weakly patients
- Common teas
- Eggnog for the sick
- Negus for the sick
- Raw egg and milk for convalescents
- Milk punch for the sick
- Milk punch, with eggs, for weak patients
- Claret punch
- Currant shrub, for the sick
- English shrub, for the sick
- Acid drinks from raspberry vinegar jelly, is nourishing and pleasant for invalids
- Toast water
- Raw egg drink for invalids, strengthening, restorative and pleasant
- Drink for great thirst of fever patients [cream of tartar, orange peel and sugar]
- Pectoral drink
- Herb teas, for the sick room
- Sage tea
- Mint teas
- Catnip tea
- Pennyroyal tea
- Gentian root
- Strawberry leaf tea
- Blackberry tea
- Mint tea, juleped
- Rice pudding, baked
- Tapioca cream pudding
- Graham pudding steamed
- Egg toast
- Pap of boiled flour, for diarrhoea of children
- Wine jelly
- Arrowroot
- Beefsteak broiled
- Mutton or lamb chops

1888

Dr Holbrook's American Cookery: With an Australian appendix of over 100 refreshing drinks for all seasons. (Holbrook, 1888) [Hoyle 639]

Advice (pp115-1440)
[General advice on practical dietetics]

Recipes (pp147-161)
- Lemonade for an invalid
- Barley water
- Apple water
- Imperial drink
- Rice water
- Beef tea (2 recipes)
- Restorative milk [isinglass, milk and sugar]
- Barley milk

The Kingswood Cookery Book (2nd edition). (Wicken, 1888) [Hoyle 1364]
Advice (pp 9-25)

Beef tea is generally the first thing called for. In severe cases of fever raw beef tea is often ordered.

Milk contains all the 40 things necessary for our system and should be given freely. All milk puddings are much lighter if the white of eggs are beaten separately and stirred in just before the pudding is baked or boiled.

Semolina and tapioca are much better than arrowroot or cornflour puddings.

Fish should form an important article of the diet in the sick room. Whiting is the least oily and most digestible.

Rabbit and game, if not too high, form a pleasant change in the bill of fare.

Purees, being rubbed through a sieve, are very easy of digestion. Vegetables too should be served this way.

As a rule, never ask a patient what he would like; so few can bear this. Rather bring a tasty, little meal as a surprise.

Recipes
- Baked milk (p20)
- Mutton broth (p41)
- Beef tea (p42)
- Raw beef tea (p42)
- Gruel (p50)
- Boudins of whiting (p63)
- Boiled chicken (p123)

1891 (3rd edition) identical recipes and advice

1898 (4th edition) (Wicken, 1898) [Hoyle 1366] Identical advice

Recipes
- Mutton broth (p45)
- Raw beef tea (p45)
- Beef tea (2 recipes) (p46)
- Boudins of whiting (p70)
- Invalid's chicken (p159)
- Savoury custard (p167)
- Egg broth (p3410)
- Toast water (p356)

1913 (6th edition) identical to 4th edition

1889

Coles Popular Cookery. (Payne, 1889) [Hoyle 1025]
Advice (pp325-328) [General advice on invalid cookery]

Recipes (pp328-334)
- Apple water
- Arrowroot jelly
- Arrowroot pudding
- Barley gruel
- Barley water
- Beef, mutton and veal broth
- Beef tea (2 recipes)
- Beef tea jelly
- Bread pudding, light
- Broth, clear
- Broth for invalids
- Broth, quickly made
- Calf's foot broth
- Calf's foot jelly
- Caudle (2 recipes)
- Chicken and veal broth

- Chicken broth
- Chicken, minced
- Chicken or fowl, to extract the essence of
- Chicken panada (2 recipes)
- Chicken with sauce
- Chicken with sippets
- Eel broth
- Egg wine
- Eggs
- Gloucester jelly
- Isinglass jelly
- Lemonade
- Lemon water
- Light puddings of vermicelli, semolina, tapioca, rice, ground rice
- Macaroni with broth
- Meat jelly, restorative
- Mutton broth (2 recipes)
- Orange jelly
- Orangeade
- Orgeat
- Panada
- Pork jelly, Dr Ratcliff's Restorative
- Shank jelly
- Sippets
- Sponge cake pudding
- Tapioca jelly
- Tench broth
- Toast water
- Veal broth (very nourishing)
- Veal, to extract the essence of
- Vermicelli, Italian paste and rice
- Water gruel (2 recipes)
- Whey
- White broths

Cassell's Shilling Cookery. (Payne, 1898) [Hoyle 1022] identical content

Cookery Recipes for the People (2nd edition). (Pearson, 1889) [Hoyle 1030]

<u>Recipes</u> (pp12-118)
- Mulled wine
- Arrowroot
- Sago
- Toast water
- Apple water
- Steak broiled
- Breast of chicken
- Digestive pudding
- Invalid's jelly
- Chicken broth
- Calf's foot broth

1894 (3rd edition) (Pearson, 1894) [Hoyle 1031]

<u>Recipes</u> (pp112-118)
- Mulled wine
- Arrowroot
- Sago
- Toast water
- Invalid pudding
- Minced steak
- Barley water
- Oatmeal gruel
- Beef tea
- Lemon drink
- Apple water
- Steak broiled
- Breast of chicken
- Digestive pudding
- Invalid's jelly
- Chicken broth
- Calf's foot broth

1890-1899

Vitadatio Sick Room Cookery Book and General Recipes (Vitadatio, 1899)

SIXPENCE.

THE ECONOMIC HOUSEWIFE'S GUIDE TO COOKERY.

BY

AN • EXPERIENCED • AUSTRALIAN • COOK.

West Maitland.
E. Tipper, Printer, near Telegraph Office,
1894.

The Economic Housewife's Guide to Cookery by An Experienced Australian Cook (May, 1894)

1890

J.G. Hanks & Co.'s Cookery Guide: The cook's compass. (Wicken, 1890b)
[Hoyle 1361]
Advice (p121)

In preparing food for invalids there are two important things to be considered; one is how to obtain the greatest amount of nourishment in a small compass; and the other is how to serve the food in an appetising manner when cooked.

The powers of digestion are always impaired during illness, care must be taken therefore that dishes served are of a digestible nature and thoroughly cooked.

Mutton and lamb are more digestible but not so nutritious as beef; veal and pork must be avoided; poultry and game are good. Fish is a valuable food; whiting and silver bream are among the most suitable as they contain the least oil. Eggs lightly cooked, and vegetables well boiled, are excellent, and semolina the finest of all pulse foods.

Recipes (pp121-133)

- Invalid's chop
- Potato soufflé
- Stewed celery
- Invalid's chicken
- Stewed chop
- Tomato omelette
- Omelette soufflé
- Calf's foot jelly
- Chicken broth
- Veal broth
- Invalid fish
- Boudins of whiting
- Cup pudding
- Sponge cake
- Lemonade
- Toast water
- Apple water
- Barley water (2 recipes)
- Rice water
- Gruel
- Black cap pudding
- Bread and butter pudding
- Tapioca and apples
- Semolina pudding

Recipes Given by Mrs Wicken at the Cookery Class, Hobart: Supplement to Kingswood Cookery Book. (Wicken, 1890a) [Hoyle 1369]
Recipe (p12)

- Invalid chop

1891

The Australian Home: A handbook of domestic economy. (Wicken, 1891)
[Not in Hoyle]
Advice (pp211-230)

The diet for an invalid and convalescent must be at once nutritious, easy of digestion, and well cooked. Raw eggs, beef tea, mutton broth, and milk are amongst the best liquid foods. In cases of typhoid fever nothing but liquids must be given until the patient has well nigh recovered, the nurse must be firm on this point, for if solid food is taken a severe relapse and often fatal consequences follow.

Fish, especially whiting, are good food to begin with when solid food is allowed, also boiled batter, semolina and bread and butter puddings. Fowls, game and mutton are the lightest animal foods. Well cooked vegetables and stewed fruits are wholesome. Oysters are the only shellfish that should be given. These should be taken raw as a rule.

Never worry a patient about what he will have to eat, this often takes away the appetite, but rather prepare some little dish and bring it as a surprise, it will often be eaten with relish, when, if it had been talked about beforehand, it would have been refused. Present only a small quantity of food at a time. If too much is given it will often take the appetite away.

No highly seasoned or made dishes must find their way into the sick room; all food should be thoroughly cooked, under-done food is always indigestible. Whether it is a cooked basin of gruel or a roast let it be thoroughly cooked. There is a great deal of difference between a slice of toast and a poached egg well and badly cooked.

There are many simple soups which are good and nourishing if properly prepared, such for instance as clear soup, macaroni soup, tapioca cream, lentil soup, semolina soup. Recipes for these and many others will be found in the Kingswood Cookery Book, and need not be given here. Only a small quantity of soup should be prepared at a time, and it should be varied from day to day.

Very little dependence must be placed on nourishment in arrowroot and cornflour, as these foods contain little else than starch. Even jelly itself is not very nourishing, but it can be made a vehicle for other foods that are nutritious. Jelly for invalids must be made from calf's feet or ox foot. The gelatine bought ready for use is very good for supper jellies, but for invalids it is much better to make the gelatine by boiling down the feet. This can form the basis of both sweet and savoury jelly.

Boiled milk with a tablespoon of brandy to every half-pint is a good restorative and much easier digestion than raw milk.

Coles Australian Household Guide; A Universal Domestic Advisor: Comprising the new and enlarged edition of Mrs. Beeton's cookery book. (Coles Book Arcade, 1891) [Hoyle 276]
Recipes (pp162-165)
- Arrowroot
- Barley gruel
- Barley water
- Beef tea (4 recipes)
- Chicken broth
- The invalid's cutlet
- Egg wine
- Gruel
- Invalid's jelly
- Lemonade for invalids
- Mutton broth
- Rice milk
- Toast water

1891 Mrs Beeton's Cookery Book and Household Guide. Dymock's Special Edition
Identical recipes to 1879 English edition

192-? Mrs Beeton's Cookery Book: All about cookery, household work, marketing, trussing, carving etc. (Beeton, 192-?) [Hoyle 143]
Recipes (pp331-333)
- Arrowroot
- Barley gruel
- Barley gruel (patent barley)
- Barley water
- Blackcurrant tea
- Curds and whey

- Egg and wine
- Eggnog
- Gruel, oatmeal
- Lemonade
- Linseed tea
- Peptonised gruel
- Rice water (Dr Pavy)
- Toast water
- White wine whey

1892

Advanced Hygiene: How to cure disease without recourse to drugs or medicine of any kind. (Hern, 1892) [Hoyle 635]

Advice (pp60-63)
[General advice on diet for the sickroom]

Recipes (pp63-67)
- Arrowroot
- Bread jelly
- Barley water
- Decoction of Carrageen moss
- Decoction of Iceland moss
- Flour and milk (particularly suitable for dysentery and diarrhoea)
- Gum water
- Lemonade
- Lemon peel tea
- Linseed tea (for pulmonary and urinary affections)
- Oatmeal gruel
- Oatmeal porridge
- Orgeat
- Rice water or mucilage of rice (irritable states of the bowel)
- Tamarind Whey (refrigerant and slight laxative)
- Toast and water
- Treacle whey, or posset (diaphoretic for a common cold)
- Barley water
- Sago milk
- Currant jelly
- Raspberry vinegar
- Apple jelly
- Sherbet cream

1893

The Art of Living in Australia. (Muskett, 1893) [Hoyle 919]

Recipes (pp268-269)
- Beef tea
- Raw beef tea

Tinned Foods and How to Use Them. (Anon, 1893) [Hoyle 1299]

Advice (pp208-209)
For invalids and children it is most necessary that food be provided of the most pure and nourishing kind. It is, as a rule, better to make the foods that require milk, with that in a condensed form. There is a prejudice in favour of fresh beef tea, but unless this be perfectly made, quite free from any sign of grease, the preparations of Liebig, Bouillon Fleet, Brand's

extract, Bovril, etc are better, as they are so clear and bright, and look tempting to those whose appetites are not large.

Recipes (pp208-228)
- Apple water (a cooling drink)
- Apricot rizine pudding
- Arrowroot jelly
- Arrowroot (milk)
- Arrowroot (water)
- Barley gruel
- Barley water (thick)
- Beef tea (3 recipes)
- Beef tea custard (Liebig's extract)
- Bouillon soup
- Brand's extract
- Cocoa cake
- Cocoa pudding
- Custards (Rizine)
- Egg drink
- Egyptian food (Symington's)
- Farola cream (a dish for invalids)
- Gruel
- Invalid's pudding (2 recipes)
- Lemon blancmange
- Lemon water (a cooling drink)
- Lemonade
- Marbled jelly
- Plain cake (2 recipes)
- Raspberry cream
- Raspberry syrup
- Rice water
- Rizine cake
- Rizine plain cake
- Rizine milk (for invalids)
- Semolina blancmange
- Wheat crystal pudding

1894

The Economic Housewife's and Beekeeper's Guide to Cookery. (May, 1894)
[Hoyle 784]
Advice (pp iv-viii)
[General preface on the chemistry of cooking]

Recipes (pp81-88)
- Beef tea (3 recipes)
- Raw beef tea
- Invalid's pudding
- Savoury custard
- Arrowroot pudding
- An invalid's egg
- Invalid's fish
- Tapioca pudding
- Chicken panada
- Egg drink
- Cream of barley
- Rice water
- Apple water
- Invalid's lemonade (for fevers)
- Sage tea
- Invalid's soup
- Gruel
- A nice substitute for gruel [made with sago and pearl barley]

1895

The Australian Enquiry Book. (Rawson, 1895) [Hoyle 1121]

Recipe (p97)
- Jelly for an invalid [stock, lemon, cloves, brandy, eggs]

Women's Missionary Association of NSW Cookery Book of Good and Tried Receipts (3rd edition). (MacInnes, 1895) [Hoyle 1061]

Recipes
- Chicken broth for invalids (p17)
- Chicken essence for invalids (p17)
- Invalid's soup (p18)

1902 (7th edition) identical to 3rd edition
1904 (8th edition) identical to 3rd edition
1906 (9th edition)

Recipes (pp207-211)
- Arrowroot made with milk
- Baked milk
- Beef essence
- Raw beef tea
- Beef tea
- Beef tea custard
- White broth
- To grill a chop
- To stew a chop (this is very easily digested)
- To boil eggs
- To boil eggs for dyspeptics
- To poach eggs
- Gruel
- Hot milk and soda water
- Baked oysters
- Fricasseed oysters
- Scalloped oysters
- Sir A. Clarke's method of making tea (this is excellent for an invalid or aged person)
- Steamed whiting

Household remedies (pp212-213)
- Linseed tea (for coughs)

1907 (10th edition) identical recipes
1909 (11th edition) identical recipes
1912 (12th edition) identical recipes
1913 (13th edition) identical recipes
1915 (14th edition) identical + albumen water
1918 (15th edition) identical recipes to 14th
1920 (16th edition) identical recipes to 14th
1922 (17th edition) identical recipes to 14th
1927 (19th edition) identical recipes to 14th
1931 (20th edition) (Women's Missionary Association of the Presbyterian Church of New South Wales, 1931) [Hoyle 1075]

Recipes (pp205-210)
- Albumen water
- Arrowroot made with milk
- Baked milk
- Beef essence
- Raw beef tea
- Beef tea
- Beef tea custard
- Chicken broth for invalids

- Chicken essence for invalids
- Invalid's soup
- White broth
- To grill a chop
- To stew a chop (this is very easily digested)
- To boil eggs
- To boil eggs for dyspeptics
- To poach eggs
- Gruel
- Hot milk and soda water
- Baked oysters
- Fricasseed oysters
- Scalloped oysters
- Sir A. Clarke's method of making tea
- Steamed whiting

1936 (21st edition) identical recipes to 20th
1944 (22nd edition) identical recipes to 20th
1950 (23rd edition) identical recipes to 20th
1962 (new edition) called The Presbyterian Cookery Book of Good and Tried Recipes. (Women's Missionary Association of the Presbyterian Church of New South Wales, 1962)

Recipes (pp224-230)

- Albumen water
- Angels' food
- Arrowroot
- Barley water
- Beef essence
- Beef tea
- Coddled egg
- Creamed fish
- Grilled fish
- Fish and eggs
- Gruel
- Hot milk and soda water
- Baked oysters
- Drink for invalids
- Egg flip
- Eggnog
- Fricasseed oysters
- Scalloped oysters
- Beef mince
- Savoury liver custard
- Junket
- Light bread pudding
- Apple soufflé
- Beef tea custard
- Raw beef tea
- Chicken broth
- Mutton broth
- Broth for invalids
- Orange drink
- To stew a chop
- Grilled chop
- Lemon drink
- Peach foam
- Milk jelly
- Tea made with milk
- Egg and milk

1979 (Revised metric edition) identical to 1962 edition. Reprinted 1983/1984/1989

1896

Diet Lists for Australian Medical Practitioners. (Springthorpe & Mullins, 1896) [Not in Hoyle]

Recipes (in 12 different diets and recipes for use in hospitals)

- Peptonised milk
- Arrowroot
- Rice milk
- Vermicelli milk soup
- Raw meat juice
- Beef tea

- Mutton broth
- Tapioca soup
- Eggnog
- Whey
- Junket
- Meat tea
- Oatmeal soup
- Gluten bread
- Bran bread
- Almond bread
- White wine whey
- Malt (ground) and rice pudding
- Flour ball
- Barley jelly
- Chicken broth
- Scotch beef broth

1897

Australian Cook and Laundry Book. (Rawson, 1897) [Hoyle 1121]
[The preface states that the material is an extract from The Australian Enquiry Book (1895)]
Recipe (p97)
- Jelly for invalids

Australian Table Dainties and Appetising Dishes. (Wicken, 1897) [Hoyle 1360]
Recipes (pp143-150)
- Claret jelly
- Toast water
- Rice water
- Apple water
- Lemonade or orangeade
- Oyster soufflé
- Restorative soup (veal/mutton/beef, onion, carrot, pepper)
- Vermicelli broth
- Fried whiting
- Batter pudding
- Rice meringue
- Sponge cakes
- Savoury omelette

Cottage Cookery (Hygienic and Economic) by "Rita" (2nd edition). (Vaile, 1897) [Hoyle 1144]
Advice (p50-51)
[General advice and instruction on Preparation of Raw Meat, Beef Tea]

Recipes (pp 51-54)
- Beef tea
- Chicken broth
- Calf's foot jelly
- Peptonised beef
- Beef juice
- Toast
- Rice water
- Barley water
- Lemonade
- Apple water
- Red or blackcurrant jelly
- Milk jelly
- Egg jelly
- Linseed tea
- Water gruel
- Rice gruel
- Oatmeal gruel

1898

The Australian Household Manual (1st edition). (Winning, 1898)[Hoyle 1388]

<u>Advice</u> (p48)

Invalid cookery is a branch in itself, requiring special care and attention. It is important that food for invalids, or very sick persons, should be light, nourishing, and easy of digestion; also, that it be given in as concentrated a form as possible, in order that the small quantity which a patient is able to take at a time may afford sufficient nourishment without taxing the stomach or digestive powers – such as, for instance, "Chicken Essence", "Raw Beef Sandwiches", "Beef Tea", "Egg Brandy" etc.

Let the food be made as appetising as possible, but carefully avoid highly seasoned dishes. Never over-sweeten any dish, as that is not only unwholesome, but nauseating, to a sick palate.

And never forget that cleanliness, and daintiness, in the manner of serving food, go far towards improving the appetite of the sick and suffering, for the life of a patient may depend upon the amount of nourishment he can be tempted to swallow.

<u>Recipes</u> (pp48-55)

- Beef tea
- Chicken broth
- Chicken essence
- Mutton broth
- Veal broth
- Minced collops
- Oysters
- Raw beef sandwiches
- Brains
- Sweetbreads
- Wine jelly
- Gruel
- Arrowroot
- Junket
- Baked milk
- Barley water
- Milk coffee
- Lemonade
- Toast water
- White wine whey
- Raw egg and milk
- Egg flip
- Celery tea (for rheumatism)
- Steamed eggs
- Refreshing drink for the sick [blackcurrant jam and water]
- Egg brandy

1899 (2nd edition) identical recipes
1899 (3rd edition) identical recipes

The Book of Diet. (Muskett, 1898) [Hoyle 922]

<u>Recipes</u> (pp279-281)

- Brandy and egg mixture
- Cherry brandy
- Egg cordial
- Port wine jelly
- Rum and milk
- Sherry and milk

A Friend in the Kitchen (1st edition). (Colcord, 1898) [Hoyle 259]
<u>Advice</u> (p109)
Food for the sick should generally be of a very simple character. It should be such as will furnish the most nourishment with the least tax on the digestive organs. It should be prepared with care and scrupulous cleanliness, well cooked, and served in the most inviting manner. Cover the tray with clean, white linen, and use the daintiest dishes the house affords.

<u>Recipes</u> (pp109-112)
- Arrowroot gruel
- Wheatmeal gruel
- Oatmeal gruel
- Rice gruel
- Milk gruel
- Onion gruel (good for colds)
- Lemonade, hot and cold
- Apple water
- Rice water
- Barley water
- Beef tea
- Chicken broth
- Beef tea and egg
- White of egg and milk
- Steamed egg
- Boiled egg
- Eggnog
- Eggnog hot
- Tapioca milk
- Arrowroot custard
- Apples and rice
- Tapioca cup pudding

1899 (3rd edition) identical to the 1st edition
1900 (4th edition)
<u>Recipes</u> (pp109-112)
- Arrowroot gruel
- Wheatmeal gruel
- Oatmeal gruel
- Rice gruel
- Milk gruel
- Onion gruel (good for colds)
- Lemonade, hot and cold
- Apple water
- Rice water
- Barley water
- Baked apple
- Haricot bean broth
- White of egg and milk (good for persons with weak digestion)
- Steamed egg
- Boiled egg
- Eggnog
- Tapioca milk
- Arrowroot custard
- Apples and rice
- Tapioca cup pudding

1902 (7th edition) identical contents to the 4th edition
1912 (14th edition) identical contents
1915 (16th edition) identical contents
1917 (17th edition) identical contents
192-? (Revised and enlarged edition) identical contents

Mrs Maclurcan's Cookery Book (2nd edition). (Maclurcan, 1898) [Hoyle 786]
<u>Recipes</u> (Numbers 289-311)
- Gruel
- Beef tea (2 recipes)
- Beef jelly
- Chicken broth
- Grilled chicken
- Chicken jelly

- Toast water
- Barley water (2 recipes)
- Mutton broth
- Steamed fish with sauce
- Savoury sago
- Savoury custard
- Beef tea with egg
- Apple water
- Egg drink
- Minced beef
- Spatchcock
- Omelette
- Light pudding (2 recipes)

1899 (3rd edition) identical recipes

1905 (6th edition) identical recipes <u>plus</u> the following

- Excellent cough mixture
- Rice water
- Linseed tea
- A gargle for sore throats
- Cure for scalds or burns

1910 (10th edition) identical recipes minus steamed fish, savoury sago, savoury custard, rice water and linseed tea

1922 (18th edition) identical to the 2nd edition

1930 (20th edition) identical to 10th edition

1899

The Goulburn Cookery Book (1st edition). (Rutledge, 1899)[Hoyle 1168]

<u>Recipes</u> (pp175-187)

- Apple water
- Arrowroot and blackcurrant drink (very good for affections of the throat)
- Arrowroot made with milk
- Arrowroot made with water
- Bacon on toast
- Barley water
- Small batter pudding
- Beef essence
- Beef tea (3 recipes)
- Raw beef tea
- Beef tea and oatmeal
- Isinglass blancmange
- Sheep's brains
- Bread and milk
- Small bread and butter pudding
- Bran tea
- Chicken broth
- Mutton broth
- Strengthening broth
- Small canary pudding
- Chicken panada
- To grill a chop
- To stew a chop
- To boil a joint of chicken
- To grill a joint of chicken
- A cup of coffee
- Savoury custard
- Cream of barley
- To boil an egg
- To poach an egg
- Egg lemonade
- Eggnog
- Fish cakes
- Fish soufflé
- Gruel (2 recipes)
- Bread jelly (it is given to babies who are unable to digest milk)
- Egg jelly
- Meat jelly
- Oatmeal jelly
- Wine jelly
- Lemonade (2 recipes)
- Linseed tea (good for a cough or weak chest)

- Milk toast
- Hot milk and soda water (good for sickness of the stomach, as a stimulant, and for chills and rigours or any weak state of the stomach)
- Baked oysters
- Fricasseed oysters
- Scalloped oysters
- Rice water
- Vanilla soufflé
- Tapioca custard
- A cup of tea
- Sir A. Clarke's method of making tea (milk tea) (excellent for an invalid or an aged person)
- Toast water
- Tripe (most digestible and very nourishing)
- Onion sauce for tripe
- Steamed whiting
- Wine whey

1905 (2nd edition) identical recipes to the 1st edition <u>plus</u> stewed apple
1906 (3rd edition) identical recipes to the 1st edition
1906 (4th edition) identical recipes to the 1st edition
1913 (13th edition) (Rutledge, 1913) [Hoyle 1176]
<u>Recipes</u> (pp175-187)

- Stewed apple
- Apple water
- Arrowroot and blackcurrant drink
- Arrowroot made with milk
- Arrowroot made with water
- Bacon on toast
- Barley water
- Small batter pudding
- Beef essence
- Beef tea
- Raw beef tea (3 recipes)
- Beef tea and oatmeal
- Isinglass blancmange
- Sheep's brains
- Bread and milk
- Small bread and butter pudding
- Bran tea
- Chicken broth
- Mutton broth
- Strengthening broth
- Small canary pudding
- Chicken panada
- To grill a chop
- To stew a chop
- To boil a joint of chicken
- To grill a joint of chicken
- A cup of coffee
- Savoury custard
- Cream of barley
- To boil an egg
- To poach an egg
- Egg lemonade
- Eggnog
- Fish cakes
- Fish soufflé
- Gruel (2 recipes)
- Bread jelly
- Egg jelly
- Meat jelly
- Oatmeal jelly
- Wine jelly
- Lemonade (2 recipes)
- Linseed tea
- Milk toast
- Hot milk and soda water
- Baked oysters
- Fricasseed oysters
- Scalloped oysters
- Rice water
- Vanilla soufflé
- Tapioca custard
- A cup of tea
- Sir A. Clarke's method of making tea

- Toast water
- Tripe
- Onion sauce for tripe
- Steamed whiting
- Wine whey

1916 (19th edition) identical recipes to the 13th edition
1920 (27th edition) identical recipes to the 13th edition
1924 (30th edition) identical recipes to the 13th edition
1926 (32nd edition) identical recipes to the 13th edition
1928 (33rd edition) identical recipes to the 13th edition
1930 (34th edition) identical recipes to the 13th edition
1934 (35th edition) identical recipes to the 13th edition
1937 (39th edition) (The New Goulburn Cookery Book). (Rutledge & McCarthy, 1937) [Hoyle 1193] [Reduced number of recipes]

Recipes (pp179-186)

- Albumen water
- Apple water
- Arrowroot or cornflour
- Cream of barley
- Barley water
- Raw beef tea
- Beef tea (2 recipes)
- Gelatine blancmange
- Sheep's brains
- Small bread and butter pudding
- Chicken broth
- Mutton broth
- Strengthening broth
- To boil a joint of chicken
- Grilled chicken
- Chicken panada
- Stewed chop
- Savoury custard
- Coddled egg
- Egg jelly
- Egg lemonade
- Eggnog
- Gruel
- Meat jelly
- Oatmeal jelly
- Wine jelly
- Lemonade
- Hot milk and soda water
- Baked oysters
- Fricasseed oysters
- Scalloped oysters
- Rice water
- Fish soufflé
- Vanilla soufflé
- Milk tea
- Toast water
- Fricasseed tripe
- Steamed whiting
- Wine whey

1975 (40th edition) Reprint of the 1st edition (1899)

Our Daily Fare and How to Provide It. (Anon, 1899a)[Hoyle 1015]
Advice (p94)
Invalids and Children should be liberally fed with Dr Ridge's Patent Food. Those whose digestions are so weak that they are unable to take anything else will find this not only strengthening and nutritious, but most soothing to the stomach and digestive organs.

The Twentieth Century Cookery Book. (Anon, 1899b) [Hoyle 239]
Recipes (pp42, 52, 61)
- Beef tea
- Mutton broth
- Savoury custard
- Raw beef tea

Vitadatio Sick Room Cookery Book and General Recipes. (Vitadatio, 1899) [Hoyle 1330]
Recipes (pp14-42)
- Beef tea (3 recipes)
- Raw beef tea
- Mutton broth
- Chicken broth
- Calf's foot broth
- Groats and oatmeal
- Barley gruel
- Onion gruel
- Porridge
- Rice water
- Barley water
- Toast water
- Apple water
- Lemonade
- Milk and soda water
- Blackcurrant and arrowroot water
- Egg brandy
- White wine whey
- Lemon jelly
- Orange jelly
- Coffee jelly
- Chicken jelly
- Claret jelly
- Savoury custard
- Toast
- Butter water toast
- Milk toast
- Cream toast
- French or egg toast
- Boiled whiting or flounder
- Grilled whiting or flounder
- Whiting, plain souchet
- Baked whiting or flounder
- Scalloped oysters
- Broiled oysters
- Oyster toast
- To blanch oysters
- Boiled eggs
- Poached eggs
- Scrambled eggs
- Omelette
- Grilled mutton chops
- Grilled chicken
- Tripe
- To blanch onions
- Brain canapés
- Roast sweetbread
- Chop en papilotte
- Braised sweetbread
- To blanch sweetbread
- Raw beef sandwich
- Stewed pigeon
- Boiled custard
- Baked custard
- Arrowroot pudding
- Cream-of-rice pudding
- Semolina pudding
- Arrowroot with milk
- Sago
- Blancmange
- Junket
- Custard cream

1900-1909

XXth Century Cooking and Home Decorating (Aronson, 1900)

The Australian Housewife's Guide to Domestic Economy (Winning, 1900)

190-?

Golden Recipes for the Use of All Ages. (W White and Co, 19-?) [Not in Hoyle]
Advice (p27)
A sick person should never be asked what they will have to eat, but bring them something suitable and unexpected. The most delicate person will find great nourishment from half an ounce of isinglass boiled in half a pint of milk and sweetened to taste.

Pluckings from Medical and Other Works/also Melbourne Economic Cookery Book (8th edition). (Anon, 19-?) [Not in Hoyle]
Advice (p35)
This kind of food should be nourishing and easy of digestion, relieving the stomach of as much work as possible. Strong soups, beef tea, raw or lightly boiled eggs will suit; also light puddings, chicken, *tender* roast beef sparingly. Fish lightly boiled is best. All shellfish should be avoided; also fish such as salmon. Oysters are easily digested and may be freely used; but they have a laxative effect when consumed in any quantity.

If weak persons are properly dieted, they would not require alcohol, which gives a temporary false strength. Good plain food given judiciously at proper intervals, served in an attractive manner, is much less expensive and more harmless.

Nothing equals milk for nourishment, if fresh and can be taken. 1 pint is equal to a good sized mutton chop, and is more nourishing than any soup. ⅛ part of lime water added will prevent its disagreeing with the most fastidious stomach. Prepare the lime water thus: Put a piece of unslacked lime into a quart water, let stand 24 hours, then filter for use.

Recipes (p35)
- Eggs flip
- Albuminised milk
- Albuminised water
- A very nourishing drink [yolk, sugar, milk & soda]
- Toast water

1900

Australian Economic Cookery Book and Housewife's Companion (2nd edition). (Story, 1900) [Hoyle 1277]
Advice (pp122-123)
Food that cannot be easily digested is of no use, and the taking of it by the patient can be productive of nothing but discomfort and the loss of future appetite. It must be given at such times as the patient has the desire for it, and in such a manner that the appearance alone will create the desire to eat. Large quantities containing little nourishment, even if taken by the patient, will only cause work to the digestive organs (which are especially weak at this time) without any beneficial result.

Food should neither be prepared or tasted before the sick and on no account presented a second time if refused the first. Gelatine and starchy foods, except as a means of conveying wine or milk and eggs, contain very little nourishment.

A cup of tea, though refreshing and often craved for by the sick, should only be looked upon as an accessory to the nourishment given and should not take the place of proper food.

Serving in small quantities and in a dainty manner will often induce an appetite. Remember that a pretty breakfast cup will hold all that is sufficient in the way of gruel etc., and there is no necessity to resort to a slop-basin for arrowroot and broth. Toast should have the crust removed and be cut in thin strips.

Recipes (pp123-134)
- Beef tea
- Mutton broth
- Chicken broth
- Semolina
- Steamed soufflés
- Arrowroot, cornflour and sago
- Gruel
- Chicken for invalids
- Grilled pigeon
- Chicken panada
- Chicken cutlet
- Sago cream soup
- Sweetbreads
- Chicken croquettes
- Fried oysters
- Milk jelly
- Beef tea custard
- Calf's foot jelly
- Oyster soufflé
- Sweet omelette
- Isinglass blancmange
- Light bread pudding
- Toast water
- Clear barley water
- Lemonade
- Orangeade
- Rice water
- Thick barley water
- Apple water

The Australian Housewife's Guide to Domestic Economy (2nd edition). (Winning, 1900) [Hoyle 1386]

Recipes (pp35-40)
- Beef tea
- Meat juice
- Egg flip
- Gruel
- Rum and milk
- Fish soup
- Celery soup
- Baked sweetbreads
- Mushrooms on toast
- Roast pigeon
- Sheep's brains
- Grilled mince on toast
- Stewed celery with white sauce
- Raw beef sandwiches
- Toast water
- White wine whey
- Chicken broth
- Barley water
- Milk coffee
- Rice soup
- Baked apples
- Invalid's pudding
- Stewed lettuce and poached egg
- Egg brandy

1902 (5th edition) identical recipes.

Cookery Class Recipes as Taught in the Kitchens of the Metropolitan Gas Company. (Ross, 1900) [Hoyle 1160]

Recipes (pp324-342)

- Beef tea (3 recipes)
- Raw beef tea
- Peptonised beef tea
- Boiled whiting or sole
- Plain whiting souchet
- Grilled whiting
- Baked whiting
- Scalloped oysters (2 recipes)
- To blanch oysters
- Oysters on toast
- Grilled chicken
- Grilled mutton chop
- Tripe
- To blanch onions
- Brain canapés
- Roast sweetbread
- Chop en papillote
- Braised sweetbread
- To blanch sweetbreads
- Raw beef sandwich
- Sago
- Chicken broth
- Rice water (2 recipes)
- Bran tea
- Barley water (2 recipes)
- Lemonade
- Toast water
- White wine whey
- Peptonised milk gruel
- Peptonised milk
- Milk and soda water
- Milk and suet
- Egg brandy (2 recipes)
- Arrowroot with wine
- Caudle
- Egg flip
- Apple tea
- Mutton tea
- Boiled flour
- Oatmeal gruel
- Wine jelly
- Calf's foot jelly
- Arrowroot pudding

XXth Century Cooking and Home Decoration. (Aronson, 1900) [Hoyle 49]

Recipes (pp269-272)

- Chicken broth with chicken and rice
- Tripe (for an invalid)
- Broiled whiting
- Beef essence
- Brown bread coffee
- Savoury gruel
- Gruel
- White wine whey
- Stewed mutton with barley
- Boiled sole
- An excellent pick-me-up [milk, gelatin, sugar and sherry]
- Rice and milk
- Chicken broth
- Chicken in jelly
- Invalid chop
- A savoury jelly
- Strengthening jelly
- Beef tea for convalescents
- Linseed tea

1901

The Commonwealth Household, Social and Medical Guide. (Curtis, 1901) [Hoyle 351]

General diet advice (103-104) including recipes for
- Toast water
- Limewater and milk

Mrs Beeton's Cookery Book: A household guide, all about cookery, household work, marketing, prices, provisions, trussing, serving, carving, menus, etc. etc. (Beeton, 1901) [Hoyle 138]

Advice (pp48-51) [General instructions on invalid cookery]

Recipe (p49)
- Beef tea

1902

The Adelaide Cookery Note Book for Domestic Economy Pupils. (Hills, 1902) [Hoyle 1256]

Recipes (pp28-29)
- Beef tea
- Custard – baked or steamed
- Linseed tea
- Apple water
- Barley water
- Lemonade
- Arrowroot
- Gruel
- To boil an egg
- Stewed chop

Australian Cookery Recipes: A handy guide for Australian housekeepers. (Wicken, 1902) [Hoyle 61]

Recipes (pp143-150)
- Claret jelly
- Toast water
- Rice water
- Apple water
- Lemonade
- Orangeade
- Vermicelli broth
- Fried whiting
- Batter pudding
- Rice meringue
- Sponge cakes
- Savoury omelette

1903

400 Tested Recipes. (McCall & McCall, 1903) [Hoyle 1104]

Recipes (pp93-97)
- A pick-me-up
- Arrowroot
- Brains and sauce
- Brain canapés
- Beef tea custard (2 recipes)
- Bread and milk
- Barley water
- Bread fritters
- Cup custard
- Chicken broth

- Chicken cutlets
- Egg broth
- Egg brandy
- Fried brains
- Fish pudding
- Fish
- Gruel
- Invalid soup
- Steamed eggs
- Stewed sweetbreads
- Tripe
- Oatmeal gruel
- Refreshing jelly
- Pineapple sponge

Colonial Everyday Cookery: Containing general rules and practical hints with carefully selected and tested recipes. (Anon, 1903) [Hoyle 277]
Advice (p227)
[General advice on invalid cooking]

Recipes (pp227-231)
- Beef tea (2 recipes)
- Beef essence (2 recipes)
- Rice flour gruel
- Oatmeal gruel
- Quaker oats with egg
- Linseed tea for colds
- Lime water (useful with milk in cases of weak digestion)
- Albumenised milk or water
- To sterilise milk
- Rice water
- Boiled or baked flour
- Chicken broth
- Chicken cream
- Egg cream
- Peach foam
- Wine jelly
- Sherry and egg
- Port wine negus
- Mulled wine
- Egg drink

Economic Cookery and Invalid Dishes. (Bile Bean, 1903) [Hoyle 160]
Advice (p25)
1. Convalescents should have small meals frequently.
2. Never keep food in the sick room.
3. Always give a patient nourishment of some kind immediately after the fatigue of dressing.
4. A few drops of brandy in a small cup of hot milk, or in two table-spoonfuls of beef tea is a useful "pick me up" for a patient faint from weakness.
5. A chicken boiled for an invalid should always be skinned before cooking.
6. Baked milk is an excellent food for an invalid.
7. Fish should always be filleted for the sick room.

Recipes (pp19-25)
- Beef tea (3 recipes)
- Beef essence
- Chicken broth
- Chickens' feet soup
- Eggs uncooked
- Oatmeal gruel
- Rice jelly
- Brandy mixture

- Beaten egg
- Sago gruel
- Milk (hot)
- Milk and lime water
- Milk toast
- Barley water
- Barley cream
- Arrowroot cream
- White broth
- Mutton broth
- Weak wine jelly
- A strong broth
- Calf's feet
- Invalid pudding
- Milk arrowroot biscuit pudding
- Invalid's jelly
- Savoury custard
- Flaxseed lemonade
- Currant water
- Hot lemonade
- Wine whey
- Whey

Elementary Cookery Book. (Miller & Miller, 1903) [Hoyle 866]
[Designed as a text for children in upper classes of State schools]
<u>Advice</u> (pp81-82)
[General advice on principles of invalid cookery]

<u>Recipes</u> (pp82-87)
- Beef tea
- Beef tea pudding
- A cup of arrowroot
- Gruel
- A cup of tea
- Coffee
- Café noir
- Cocoa
- Lemonade
- Toast water
- Clear barley water
- Thick barley water
- Blackcurrant tea
- Lime water
- Curry custard
- Tapioca cream
- Steamed fish
- Apple soufflé
- Apple pudding

1904

Home Cookery for Australia: All tested recipes (1st edition). (Presbyterian Women's Missionary Union of Victoria, 1904) [Hoyle 1091]
<u>Recipes</u> (pp144-146)
- Arrowroot jelly
- Albumen water
- Barley water
- Beef tea
- Beef tea custard
- Boiled milk
- Calf's foot broth
- Calf's foot jelly
- Calf's foot stewed
- Cream of barley
- Gruel
- Invalid blancmange
- Invalid's pudding
- Milk for invalids
- Rabbit or chicken jelly
- Restorative jelly
- Souchet fish

1906 (2nd edition) (Presbyterian Women's Missionary Union of Victoria, 1906) [Hoyle 1092]

Advice (pp159-160)

Gelatine and starch foods, except as means of conveying wine, or milk or eggs, contain very little nourishment.

Serving in small quantities and in a dainty manner will often induce an appetite.

[Various instructions including: "Avoid making little noises such as rustling the leaves of a book or clicking of knitting needles"]

Recipes (pp160-165)
- Albumen water
- Apple water
- Arrowroot jelly
- Barley water (2 recipes)
- Beef tea (2 recipes)
- Beef tea custard
- Boiled milk
- Calf's foot broth
- Calf's foot jelly
- Calf's foot stewed
- Cream of barley
- Cream chicken
- Chicken puree
- Egg foam
- Fish custard
- Good soup for an invalid
- Hot drink for a cold
- Gruel
- Invalid blancmange
- Invalid's pudding
- Milk for invalids
- Milk jelly
- Rabbit or chicken jelly
- Restorative jelly
- Semolina cream
- Souchets fish
- Toast water
- Whey
- White egg flip
- Wine for invalids

1909 (3rd edition) identical recipes
1913 (4th edition) identical recipes
1918 (5th edition) identical recipes

1905

600 Tested Recipes. (Auburn Methodist Church, 1906) [Hoyle 843]

Recipe (p133)
- Egg drink for invalid

Principles of Practical Cookery for School Pupils. (Rankin, 1905) [Not in Hoyle]

Advice (p27)

9 Rules to be observed when cooking for invalids:
1. Exercise the utmost care in the choice of food and the care of cookery utensils.
2. Follow medical instructions with regard to quantity and nature of food given.
3. Prepare only small quantities of food at one time, but let that little be nourishing.
4. Avoid over-flavouring or over-seasoning food, and if there is any risk of pepper &c. irritating the patient, do not use them at all.

5. Arrange all food as daintily as possible, in order to induce appetite. The tray for an invalid should be covered with a clean tray-cloth; the dishes used should be the prettiest available; a spray of flowers laid on the tray will help make it look bright. Cups or glasses should be filled only within an inch of the top, to avoid spilling.
6. Remove all traces of food immediately a meal is finished, and never present food a second time that the patient has once refused.
7. Stimulating beverages should never be given without the express instructions from the doctor, and even tea and coffee should be avoided after 5p.m., so the patient's rest may not be interfered with.
8. All meals must be served punctually, and arrangements made so that the food will not be spoiled either by over-cooking or re-heating, nor the patient's appetite be interfered with by delay in serving meals.
9. Be careful to remove all traces of fats from broths &c. If it is impossible to remove it all before cooking, it should be skimmed off before serving.

Milk is often the only food supplied during the acute stages of illness, as very little food is needed. During convalescence the patient must be well nourished, but whenever possible it is advisable to provide variety in the diet, so that the appetite might be stimulated.

1907

Good Health Cookery Book. (Kress, 1907) [Hoyle 742]

<u>Advice</u> (pp109-112)

There is no branch of cookery more important than the preparation of food for the sick. It should always be the aim of the one preparing the foods to supply the required amount of building material to supply the waste which is taking place in the body. A food may be excellent for a person in health, and yet improper food for the sick, because it would tax the weakened digestive organs too much to convert the material for the blood and tissues.

Food for the sick must be palatable, nutritious and easily digested. To select such food requires some knowledge of foods, their dietetic value, and the physiology of the body, as well as the nature of the illness with which the patient is suffering. This knowledge should be a part of the education of every woman, no matter to what class of society she belongs.

As far as possible the food should be a surprise to the one who is ill.

In cases of fever it is always best during the first 24 to 48 hours to withhold food altogether, giving the patient freely of distilled or well-boiled water, to encourage elimination of waste, which nature is trying to get rid of. This simple precaution arrests what would be a run of sickness of several weeks. Do not be too anxious in urging food upon a patient. Nature is a wise guide, and can, as a rule, be relied upon at this period. The appetite is taken away for a wise purpose.

<u>Recipes</u> (pp112-113)
- Barley gruel
- Oatmeal gruel
- Gluten gruel
- Raisin gruel
- Granose gruel
- Vegetable broth
- Mixed vegetable broth
- Tomato gluten
- Malted nut broth
- Malted nut bouillon
- Maltose cream

1909 Identical recipes

1908

The Attainment of Health and the Treatment of the Different Diseases by Means of Diet. (Muskett, 1908) [Hoyle 921]

Advice (pp319-322)

[General advice on diet in convalescence from fevers and feverish conditions (as well as recovery from other acute diseases) allows the following foods]:

- Bread and milk
- Arrowroot
- Cornflour
- Rice flour
- Sago
- Semolina
- Tapioca
- Raw oysters
- Boiled fish
- Boiled chicken
- Soft boiled egg
- Asparagus
- Cauliflower
- Vegetable marrow
- Brains
- Calf's foot
- Calf's head
- Sheep's tongue
- Sweetbread
- Tripe
- French beans
- Mashed potato
- Stewed celery
- Boiled custard
- Milk pudding
- Stewed fruit.

Advice (p581)

The great prominence which is now accorded to all matters connected with diet and food is one of the most striking features of modern medicine.

In all forms of acute diseases, the administration of suitable nourishment is of the utmost importance. A patient, after coming through an exhausting illness is, likewise, in need of the most restorative articles, in order to regain strength and vitality.

Recipes (pp581-678)

- Acorn cocoa (exceedingly valuable in the treatment of diarrhoeal and other bowel diseases, occurring in infants and young children)
- Albumen water (mostly required in cases accompanied by debility, exhaustion or prostration)
- Almond drink (soothing in colds on the chest, bronchitis and inflammation of the lungs)
- Apple drink (specially recommended for all fevers and feverish conditions)
- Artificial meat juice (administered in anaemia, fevers and feverish conditions, gastric ulcer, gastritis and vomiting associated with purging)
- Barley water
- Beef tea (2 recipes)
- Brandy and egg mixture
- Bread
- Caraway water
- Chicken broth
- Cinnamon water
- Egg cordial
- Egg with brandy
- Gelatine and milk
- Gum water and sherry
- Honey and milk
- Imperial drink
- Lemon drink
- Lemon sponge
- Lime water
- Linseed tea

47

- Malt soup
- Milk, diabetic
- Milk porridge
- Mutton broth
- Parkin [oatmeal and flour cake]
- Peptonised milk
- Peptonised beef tea
- Peptonised milk gruel
- Phosphoric acid drink
- Port wine jelly
- Raw meat juice
- Raw meat mince
- Raw meat pulp
- Raw meat soup
- Rice water
- Sherry and milk
- Sugar water
- Toast water
- Veal broth
- Whey, plain
- White of egg solution

Hobart Cookery Book of Tested Recipes, Household Hints and Home Remedies. (Committee of Ladies for the Methodist Central Mission Melville Street Hobart, 1908) [Hoyle 838]

Recipes (pp139-141)

- Barley water
- Beef tea custard for invalid
- Beef tea custards (This is very nourishing)
- Eggs for dyspeptics (Some doctors say eggs cooked for 30 minutes are even more easily digested)
- Baked milk
- Effervescing gruel (This will counteract a chill and help produce sleep)
- Fried brains
- Fried sweetbreads
- Tripe cutlets
- Invalid tea
- Most nourishing was to boil rice
- Raw meat juice
- Toast water
- Sheep's brains

1912 (3rd **edition**) identical recipes plus Scrambled brains
192-? (4th **edition**) identical recipes
1946 (9th **edition**) identical recipes
1949 (10th **edition**) identical recipes
1952 (10th **edition**) identical recipes
1961 (11th **edition**) identical recipes

The Public School Girls' Book of Recipes. (Teachers of the West Redfern Cookery School, 1908) [Hoyle 1348]

Recipes (pp47-50)

- Raw beef tea
- Beef tea (2 recipes)
- Toast water
- Gruel
- Barley water (2 recipes)
- Rice water
- Chicken broth
- Mutton broth
- Lemonade

WMU Cookery Book of over 588 Tried Recipes (7th edition). (The Queensland Presbyterian Missions, 1908) [Hoyle 1082]
Recipes (pp131-134)
- Apple water
- Oatmeal drink
- Pudding for an invalid
- Baked apples
- Steamed apples
- Beef tea
- Beef tea custard
- Cup custard
- Milk jelly
- Steamed whiting
- Baked whiting or bream
- Invalid dish of fish

1930 (14th edition) identical recipes to the 7th edition plus:
- Barley water – for infants or invalids
- Toast water
- Calf's foot jelly
- Celery tea (for rheumatism)

1944 (16th edition) identical to 14th edition
1961 (19th edition) No invalid cookery recipes

1909

The Albion Park Scotch Fair Cookery Book. (Miller, 1909) [Hoyle 867]
Recipes (pp17-19)
- Milk diluted for invalids
- Beef tea
- Chicken broth
- Boiled brains
- Stewed tripe
- Boiled chicken
- Peptonised oysters
- Jelly for invalids
- Arrowroot
- Gruel
- Porridge

Guild Cookery Book. (Ladies Working Guild, 1909). [Hoyle 640]
Recipes (pp87-88)
- Egg on toast
- Egg cooked in milk
- A soothing cough mixture
- Savoury milk
- Beaten egg and milk
- Mutton broth
- Steamed eggs
- A nourishing cup of tea
- Jelly for invalids

Home and Health: A household manual. (A Competent Committee of Home-makers and Physicians, 1909) [Hoyle 641]
Advice (p516)
Some people have the erroneous idea that "something to tempt the appetite" is the first remedy of all diseases. On the contrary, however, it is usually the case that the appetite has "been tempted" too much. Instead of giving up rich indigestible dishes for the sick, better allow them to fast for a day or two, until nature has had time to rid itself of the accumulated poisons which have caused the trouble. Food should not be urged upon the sick. Nature will

usually demand it as soon as it is needed; and when food is given it should be simple and plain. Patients recovering satisfactorily from a long illness have died in a few hours by being permitted to eat heartily of solid food.

The Schauer Cookery Book (1st edition). (Schauer & Schauer, 1909)[Hoyle 1214]
No invalid cookery information
1912 (3rd edition) No invalid cookery information
1918. The Schauer Cookery Book: With which is incorporated The Invalid Cookery Book (4th edition). (Schauer, 1918)
Section pp434-512 identical to text in "Cookery for Invalids" (Schauer & Schauer, 1912)
1931. The Schauer Improved Cookery Book. (Australian and 7th edition).
No invalid cookery information
1946 (9th edition). Continuation of The Schauer Cookery Book called: The Schauer Australian Cookery Book. (Schauer & Leese, 1946) [Hoyle 1221]
[Includes a new section on Invalid Cookery]

Advice (pp578-579)
The diet of an invalid, especially while convalescing, must be well balanced, that is built on the Protective Foods which are so vital to build up and maintain a healthy body. They are milk, eggs, meat, fish, vegetables, fruit, bread, butter and cheese. [General advice on basic nutrition follows]

Specimen menus (pp580-582)
[Suggested dishes for each meal of the day, with additional options in Winter]

Recipes (p582-599)
- Albumenised water or milk
- Arrowroot
- Baked milk
- Barley water (2 recipes)
- Bread jelly
- Chicken jelly
- Gruel
- Invalid savoury jelly
- Meat jelly
- Oatmeal jelly
- Chicken broth for invalids
- Giblet broth
- Mutton broth
- Sheep's head broth
- Veal broth
- Beef tea (2 recipes)
- Beef essence
- Beef juice
- Pure beef juice
- Raw beef tea (contains food value)
- Fortified beef tea (food value)
- Milk beef tea
- Beef tea custard
- Beef cakes
- Invalid soup
- Sago cream soup
- Black currant tea
- Lemon drink
- Orange drink (vitamins A, B & C)
- Pineapple drink
- Raw tomato juice
- Boiled egg for invalids
- Coddled eggs
- Cream egg
- Plain steamed egg
- Poached egg
- Scrambled egg
- Egg flip
- Fish au gratin
- Fish and tomatoes

- Fried fillets of whiting in egg batter
- Grilled fillets of whiting
- Steamed whiting
- Creamed fish
- Fish scrambled
- Fried fish
- Brains
- Grilled chops or steak
- Kidneys
- Liver
- Tripe
- Sweetbread
- Invalid mince
- Grilled mince
- Chicken, rabbit or veal cream
- Quenelles
- Chicken fillet steamed (suitable for invalid or convalescent)
- Various meals for an invalid from one chicken or fowl)
- Steamed mutton chop
- Baked mutton chop
- Plain omelette (savoury)
- Cheese omelette
- Oysters devilled
- Oysters scalloped
- Peptonised foods
- Salmon salad
- Sweet or savoury soufflé
- Apple soufflé
- Apple blancmange
- Baked apple
- Steamed apple
- Baked custard
- Steamed custard
- Fruit foam
- Invalid pudding
- Junket
- Light bread and butter custard
- Milk jelly
- Sago cream
- Wine jelly
- Rusks
- Cerevite rusks
- Zwieback (twice baked bread)
- Bran biscuits
- Raw beef sandwiches
- Liver sandwiches

1956 (11th edition) identical to the 9th edition

1910-1919

The Kookaburra Cookery Book (Committee of the Lady Victoria Buxton Girls' Club, 1915)

The War Chest Cookery Book (The War Chest Fund, 1917)

191-?

Cookery Instruction Card: Set of 33 cards. (Victoria Department of Public Instruction, 191-?) [Not in Hoyle]

Advice (Card 26)

The following are the diets generally ordered:
- Ordinary and Full Diet – consists of meat, bread, vegetables, etc, in variety
- Low Diet – Liquids such as tea, weak broth, barley water, thin gruel, arrowroot etc
- Milk Diet – Milk, arrowroot, sago, tapioca, rice, bread etc
- Vegetable Diet – Meat is dispensed with, fish and fowl being, however, generally allowed occasionally
- Meat Diet – Meat, cheese, eggs, milk, beef tea, broth etc.

Recipes (Cards 26 & 27)
- Beef tea (2 recipes)
- Toast water
- Cup custard
- Gruel
- Thick barley water
- Arrowroot

The Windsor Recipe Book: Containing 600 recipes. (Anon, 191-?) [Not in Hoyle]

Recipes (pp71-73)
- Sago cream and extract of beef
- Invalid jelly
- Restorative jelly
- Beef tea custard
- Essence of beef
- Sardinian soup
- Mutton jelly
- Gruel
- Oysters stewed
- Minced fowl and egg
- Rabbit soup

1910

Cassell's Household Cookery. (Heritage, 1910) [Hoyle 633]

Advice (pp1056-1058)

Rules for invalid cookery:
1. Serve everything in small quantities, appetising in appearance, and scrupulously clean.
2. Animal food, as a rule, should be fresh, particularly for dishes such as beef tea.
3. Fish should be chosen with care. White fish is the most digestible; whiting is first favourite. Shell fish and oily fish are generally forbidden and must not be given except by permission of the doctor. Oysters are an exception to this rule; they are very digestible in the raw state, but the reverse is the case if cooked.
4. If vegetables are allowed they must be fresh, cleaned, and cooked thoroughly.
5. Fruit should be ripe and sound; if over-ripe it may be as hurtful as unripe.
6. Salt, pepper and spices of all sorts must be used with extreme caution. Store sauces and the like are seldom allowed in the sick room or until convalescence sets in.
7. Eggs and milk must be fresh. The latter should be kept lightly covered for fear of dust. It should be scalded or boiled as the doctor may direct.
8. Pastry, new bread, and cakes are, speaking broadly, amongst the things that should not be given. Twice cooked meat comes under the same head. So does cheese.

9. Fried food is not good for the sick or any whose digestive powers are feeble. Freedom from fat is the thing to aim at.
10. In certain diseases *solid* feed is forbidden. Violation of this rule may mean death.
11. Sugar is best added in small quantities. It is easy to put in more, but an over-dose at first may render a dish uneatable for some patients have a great aversion to anything sweet. Saccharin is often preferred.
12. Always carry up any food, whether hot or cold, covered.
13. Try to prepare little surprises of a suitable kind for the patient, who as a rule, *should not be consulted* with regard to the diet. Monotony must be guarded against.
14. Tea should not stand many minutes; coffee must be clear and pure; cocoa should be made from nibs, or the best powder used.
15. Bulk does not imply nutriment; and cost is not indication of true food value.

Advice on Pre-digested foods (pp1058-1059):
In severe illnesses the patient is often not able to digest food of any kind without some assistance. This is owing to lack of the digestive juices. Certain foods can be digested outside the body and the patient may be tided over a critical period. Thus it is easy to make milk, beef tea, gruel etc perfectly digestible. The foods may be either *peptonised* by the aid of "peptonising powders", or *pancreatised* by the assistance of "liquor pancreaticus". "Pancreatic extract" is another name for a similar article.

Recipes (pp1065-1092)
- Apple water
- Arrowroot
- Barley custard soup
- Barley gruel
- Barley water
- Beef essence
- Beef jelly
- Beef juice
- Beef tea (2 recipes)
- Beef tea, raw
- Beef tea with tapioca
- Boiled flour
- Bread and milk
- Broth
- Brown soup
- Calf's foot jelly
- Calf's foot in milk
- Carrot and bread soup
- Cereal pudding with eggs
- Chicken dishes
- Chicken puree
- Chocolate gruel
- Cream
- Cream sauce for fish
- Cutlet, boned
- Eel broth
- Eggs
- Egg creams
- Eggs, poached
- Eggs, steamed
- Fish pudding
- Fish soufflé
- Flour, baked
- Fowl soup, from an old bird
- Fruit drinks
- Gruel, effervescing
- Iceland moss jelly
- Imperial drink
- Isinglass fruit jelly
- Lemonade
- Lemonade syrup
- Lemon tea
- Lentil flour gruel
- Light puddings
- Linseed tea
- Malt bread and milk pudding

- Malted cereal pudding
- Malted gruel
- Meat extracts
- Milk and beef tea
- Milk with chicken or mutton tea
- Milk with egg and beef tea
- Milk with meat juice
- Minced meat
- Mixed meats soup
- Mixed meats tea
- Mock omelette or puffed pudding
- Mock turtle soup
- Mutton broth
- Mutton tea
- Nourishing soup
- Oatmeal gruel
- Oatmeal milk gruel
- Oatmeal jelly
- Oatmeal thickening for beef tea etc
- Onion gruel
- Onion soup
- Orangeade
- Oysters, nourishing dishes of
- Port wine jelly
- Possets
- Potatoes
- Potted meats for sandwiches
- Puddings
- Restorative gruel or jelly
- Rice jelly
- Rice soup
- Rice water
- Rusk pudding
- Sandwiches
- Savoury blancmange
- Savoury custard
- Savoury pudding
- Sheep's feet jelly
- Solid coffee, chocolate or tea
- Suet milk
- Thickened milk
- Toast, savoury and nourishing
- Toast water
- Tripe, stewed
- Vermicelli pudding
- Vermicelli soup
- Vermicelli jelly or soup
- Whey
- Whiting, a savoury dish of

Miss Fowler's Cook Book (1st edition). (Fowler, 1910) [Hoyle 544]

Advice (pp228-229)

The food should be of such a nature that it may be readily assimilated into the system without severely taxing the digestive organs, which, in sickness, are never very strong.

The food should be varied as much as possible, for the patient is naturally restricted in his choice of diet, and, consequently, tires of the same food quickly, if prepared time after time in the same manner.

Two Golden Rules to be observed by the nurse are:

"Give a little food at a time, but give it often"

"Serve it up in as dainty and tempting a manner as possible"

Recipes (pp229-243)
- Beef tea (2 recipes)
- Raw beef tea
- Beef tea jelly
- Beef tea custard
- Mutton broth
- Invalid broth
- Veal broth
- Celery cream soup

- Sago cream soup
- Chicken soup
- Egg flip
- Milk and rum
- Egg and brandy milk
- Toast water
- Barley water (2 recipes)
- Rice water
- Treacle posset
- Linseed tea
- Cream of tartar
- Suet milk
- Apple water
- White wine whey
- Home made lemonade
- Orangeade
- Arrowroot water
- Wine arrowroot
- Gruel
- Sago gruel
- Savoury sago
- Restorative jelly
- Orange jelly
- Rabbit or chicken jelly
- Tea cup pudding
- Light bread pudding
- Tapioca custard
- Milk jelly from cow-heel

1918 (3rd edition) (Sagasco Cookery Book on cover) identical recipes to 1st edition

1923 (4th edition) identical recipes plus:
- Siegel's syrup
- Gran bits baked pudding
- Gran bits steamed pudding

The "New Idea" Cook Book: Containing over 600 recipes tested and proved good. (White, 1910) [Hoyle 490]

Recipes (pp94-100)
- Strengthening broth
- Mutton broth
- Beef tea
- Beef tea jelly
- Oysters
- Fried oysters
- Pigs in blankets
- Stewed sheep trotters
- Ragout of sweetbreads
- Brain cutlets
- Stewed rabbit
- Tripe
- Tripe cutlets
- To poach an egg
- Steamed eggs
- Omelette
- Spatchcock
- Chicken broth
- To grill a joint of chicken
- Chicken custard
- Chicken panada
- Peach foam
- Lemon sponge
- Caramel cream
- Arrowroot
- Tapioca cream
- Junket
- Boiled custard
- Lemon jelly
- Calf's foot jelly
- Barley water
- To prepare lime water (is strengthening if taken internally and is splendid for digestion)
- Toast water
- Lemonade
- Albumenised milk
- Refreshing drink for the sick [blackcurrant jam and water]

1911

Cookery for Common Ailments.
(A Fellow of the Royal College of Physicians & Browne, 1911) [Not in Hoyle]

Advice (pp ix-x)

At the end of the book there will be found a number of recipes for the preparation of foods suitable to illness in its more acute stages; these constitute "liquid or slop diet", and to these recourse may be had if it be necessary to feed the patients before the arrival of the doctor; also, with his sanction, selection may be made therefrom during the course of the illness

With this exception, no attempt is made to guide the feeding of the sick: this must be in the hands of the medical attendant. Very curious notions prevail among the uninitiated in this respect; and the doctor who should diet his patient and omit the prescription sacred to Jupiter, would incur serious risk to his reputation. Yet the diet alone may be at fault and simple regulations as to this all that is needful. The days of our Fairy Tales are not quite forgotten, and when all is said and done, the most matter-of-fact amongst us dearly loves a little mystery. Drugs have their place, and, in our opinion, a most important place; but diet in all cases takes precedence.

May we anticipate the critic, and add that a treatise in the present small compass cannot present the reader with dietetic intricacies, not to say eccentricities, but must restrict itself to teachings which have a more general currency. If these fail, the diet must be changed unhesitatingly and the organism humoured, however unorthodox or whimsical its tastes. The Science of diet has yet to be written; till that time we must leave room for the eclecticism of the palate, and admit the fancy diet.

Recipes (pp274-298)

- Beef tea (5 recipes)
- Beef tea with egg
- Beef juice
- Mutton broth
- Veal broth
- Chicken broth
- Chicken and rice broth
- Chicken milk
- Chicken broth made from giblets
- Veal and tapioca broth
- Oyster broth
- Onion soup
- Rice cream soup
- Tapioca cream soup
- Vegetable soup
- Apple soup
- Clear soup
- Celery soup
- Artichoke soup
- Asparagus soup
- Whey
- Beef jelly
- Chicken jelly
- Wine jelly
- Citric acid jelly
- Iceland moss jelly
- Irish moss jelly
- Ivory dust jelly
- Hartshorn jelly
- Lemon jelly
- Orange jelly
- Coffee jelly
- Tea jelly
- Fresh fruit jelly
- Tapioca jelly
- Arrowroot jelly
- Arrowroot blancmange
- Tapioca custard
- Tapioca cream
- Blancmange
- Superior gruel
- Plain gruel

- Barley gruel
- Barley water
- Arrowroot
- Rice caudle
- Toast water
- Toast water and cream
- Rice water
- Lemonade
- Milk lemonade
- Apple water
- Milk and soda water
- Fruit juice and soda water
- Coffee and soda water
- Egg beaten up with brandy, wine or milk
- Mulled wine and egg
- White of egg and milk
- Egg lemonade
- Egg soup
- Egg gruel
- Egg cordial
- Egg drink

The Coronation Cookery Book. (Wilson, 1911) [Hoyle 1384]
Recipe (pp178-179)
- Nutritious beef for invalids

The Keeyunga Cookery Book. (McGowan, 1911) [Hoyle 823]
Recipes (pp43-51)
- Beef juice
- Chicken jelly
- Hot milk
- Apple meringue
- Boiled custard
- Baked custard
- Baked fruit
- Beef tea (2 recipes)
- A very strengthening broth
- Cream of barley
- Savoury custard
- Port wine jelly
- Filleted whiting
- Stewed calf's foot
- Mutton cutlet
- Arrowroot gruel
- Oatmeal gruel
- Quickly made beef essence
- To sterilise milk
- Digestible flour
- Chicken broth
- Egg cream
- Fruit cream
- Egg flip
- Chicken cream
- Brandy mixture
- An excellent tonic
- Slippery elm bark tea
- Milk punch
- Irish moss lemonade
- Irish moss jelly
- Wine whey
- Baked milk
- Koumiss or milk champagne
- Snow pudding
- Gruel

The Kookaburra Cookery Book of Culinary and Household Recipes and Hints. (Committee of the Lady Victoria Buxton Girls' Club, 1911) [Hoyle 724]

Recipes (pp249-250)
- Raw beef tea
- Beef tea for the very weak
- White wine soup
- Chicken broth for invalids
- Calf's foot jelly for invalids
- Invalid jelly
- Water gruel
- Arrowroot sponge
- Cream of barley
- Steamed fish

1911 (2nd edition) identical recipes
1915 (2nd edition) identical recipes
1929 (2nd edition) identical recipes

A Small Collection of Plain Cookery Recipes: For household use. (Bishop, 1911) [Hoyle 162]

Recipes (pp41-46)
- Beef tea (2 recipes)
- Raw beef tea
- Essence of beef
- Eggnog
- Rice water
- Lemon drink
- Barley water
- Arrowroot pudding
- Steamed fish
- Egg and soda water
- Beef tea custard
- Blancmange
- Arrowroot jelly
- Toast water
- Wine whey
- Lemon whey
- Arrowroot

1912

Cookery for Invalids: For hospital and home, nurses in training schools, in private practice, and others who tend the sick. (2nd edition). (Schauer & Schauer, 1912) [Hoyle 1209]

Advice (pp5-16) [General advice on cookery for invalids includes 14 rules]:
1. Serve everything in small quantities, appetising in appearance, and scrupulously clean.
2. The food should be kept in a well-ventilated place. Animal food should be fresh. The very best of food should be selected.
3. Fish should be chosen with care; it must be fresh; white fish is the most digestible.
4. If vegetables are allowed, they must be fresh, cleaned and cooked thoroughly. When forbidden they must never be given as much harm might result.
5. Fruit should be sound and ripe.
6. Salt and pepper and spices of all sorts must be used with extreme caution.
7. Eggs and milk must be fresh.
8. Pastry, new bread, and cakes are amongst the things that should not be given. Twice cooked meat and cheese come under the same head.
9. Fried food is not good for the sick or anyone whose digestive powers are feeble.
10. In certain diseases solid food is forbidden. Violation of this rule may mean death.

11. Sugar is best added in small quantities … but too much may render the dish uneatable, for some patients have a great aversion to anything sweet.
12. Always carry up any food, whether hot or cold, covered.
13. Try to prepare little surprises for the patient, who as a rule should not be consulted as regard to diet. Monotony must be guarded against.
14. Drinks; let the hot be hot and cold be cold.

Recipes (pp59-77)

- Lime water
- Linseed tea
- Rice water
- Toast water
- Apple water
- Lemonade
- Suet milk
- Barley water – infusion
- Decoction – barley
- Gruel
- Savoury gruel
- Arrowroot
- Lemon whey
- Wine whey
- Whey
- Calf's foot in milk
- Egg arrowroot
- Cup arrowroot
- Wine arrowroot
- Oatmeal jelly
- Onion gruel
- Cow heel in milk
- Poached egg
- Steamed egg
- Egg snow
- Egg and brandy
- Baked egg
- Scrambled egg
- Egg in gravy
- Egg flip
- Savoury pudding
- Omelette
- Fish omelette
- Fish soufflé
- Apple soufflé
- Chicken and oyster soufflés
- Mock omelette or puffed pudding
- Sponge cake
- Sponge sandwich
- Small sponge cakes
- Corn flour cakes
- Madeira cakes
- Rusks
- Pulled bread
- Puddings
- Steamed milk puddings
- Baked custard pudding
- Bread-crumb pudding
- Baked bread and butter pudding
- Boiled batter pudding
- Boiled custard
- Baked apple
- Apple cream
- Stewed apples
- Isinglass blancmange
- Arrowroot pudding
- Arrowroot and apple pudding
- Isinglass fruit jelly
- Lemon sponge
- Junket
- Vermicelli pudding
- Macaroni pudding
- Malt bread pudding
- Rice and milk
- Rice pudding
- Rice custard
- Rice jelly (2 recipes)
- Rusk pudding
- Steamed batter pudding
- Baked batter pudding
- Stewed prunes
- Tapioca cream

- Tapioca pudding
- Sago pudding
- Stewed fruit
- Soufflé plain
- Semolina pudding
- Savoury pudding
- Vanilla cream
- Benger's food
- Boiled rice

Every Woman's Domestic Companion: A book of household requirements, over 700 useful recipes including paper bag cookery. (Anon, 1912) [Hoyle 489]

Recipes (various pages)
- Rice water (p65)
- Oatmeal drink (p66)
- Chicken broth for invalids (p108)
- Beef tea (p177)

Invalid and Convalescent Cookery: A collection of tried recipes for the use of Australian nurses (1st edition). (Harriott, 1912) [Hoyle 623]

Advice (ppvii-ix)

In preparing this book for the use of nurses and those engaged in attending the sick and convalescent I have endeavoured to make the quantities as small as possible so as to avoid waste by cooking too much at once. Seasonings and flavourings must be most carefully regulated. Even in cooking for those in good health flavour should never predominate, and in illness the palate is very sensitive.

There is no form of cooking that requires more thought and care than that intended for the diet of the sick and convalescent. The choice of food is often a most difficult question, for what is good for one person is not of necessity good for another, even if suffering from the same complaint.

The doctor's orders as regards diet should be most carefully carried out. Much depends on keeping up the patient's strength, and the nurse should see that sufficient food of the best kind is given in the most appetizing and nourishing form. Certain methods of cooking are quite inadmissible, and certain foods, such as pork, veal, the richer kinds of fish and pastry, must not be given.

Recipes (pp1-80)
- Barley water
- Apple water
- Rice water
- Toast water
- Lemonade
- Eggnog or beaten egg
- Gruel
- Cocoa
- Mulled wine
- Wine whey
- Whey
- Beef tea (3 recipes)
- Raw beef tea
- Beef tea custard
- Mutton broth
- Chicken broth
- Celery soup
- Julienne soup
- Fish soup
- Oyster soup
- Steamed fish
- Fried fish
- Grilled fish
- Scalloped oysters

- Oyster cream
- Fish cakes (salmon)
- Salmon croquettes
- Scalloped salmon
- Fish soufflé
- Steamed whiting with oysters
- Boiled egg
- Poached egg
- Scrambled egg
- Sweet soufflé omelette
- Savoury omelette (2 recipes)
- Egg croquette
- Frothed egg
- Lamb's sweetbreads
- Creamed sweetbreads
- Sweetbread salad
- Brain cakes
- Scalloped brains
- Fried brains
- Fricasseed brains
- Brains in potato cases
- Stewed tripe
- Grilled steak or chop
- Fricasseed chop
- Rissoles
- Cutlets
- Fricasseed tongues
- Rolled bacon on toast
- Minced meat on toast
- Savoury jelly
- Chicken croquette
- Chicken stewed in milk
- Chicken cutlet
- Roast chicken and bread sauce
- Chicken cream
- Cold chicken in white jelly
- Scalloped chicken
- Stewed apples
- Stewed quinces
- Stewed pears
- Baked apple
- Apples in jelly
- Prune jelly
- Prune shape
- Apricot gateau (2 recipes)
- Apple snow
- Boiled custard
- Small isinglass blancmange
- Steamed batter pudding
- Lemon sponge
- Lemon or wine jelly
- Calf's foot jelly
- Apricots or peach sponge cake
- Vanilla soufflé
- Canary pudding
- Sago cream
- Tapioca cream
- Custard shape
- Apple delight
- Baked milk puddings
- Baked custard (2 recipes)
- Bread soufflé
- Sago custard
- Rice pudding with egg
- Rice pudding without egg
- Tapioca custard
- Potato croquettes
- Chop potatoes
- Boiled rice
- Stewed celery
- Cauliflower
- Marrow
- Asparagus
- Broad beans
- Peas
- Beans
- Spinach
- Artichokes
- Carrots, turnips and parsnips
- Egg sandwiches
- Oyster cream sandwiches
- Fish sandwiches
- Meat sandwiches
- Tomato sandwiches (2 recipes)
- Raw meat sandwiches
- Sponge cake

- Swiss roll
- Plain cake
- Scones
- Bread and milk
- Arrowroot with milk
- Junket
- Braised quail
- Marinaded steak with olives
- Anchovy and olive savoury
- Sardine toast
- Stuffed tomatoes
- Ham toast
- Fried kidneys on toast
- Minced kidney

1922 (2nd edition). (Harriott, 1922) [Hoyle 624]

<u>Recipes</u> (pp15-76)

- Almond and apple sandwiches
- American barley water
- Apple and chicken salad
- Apple and rice meringue
- Apple, baked
- Apple, date and nut salad
- Apple in jelly
- Apple snow
- Apple water
- Apricot gateau (2 recipes)
- Artichoke soufflé
- Bacon on toast
- Baked apple
- Baked custard (2 recipes)
- Barley water
- Batter pudding, steamed
- Beaten egg
- Beef tea custard
- Beef tea (2 recipes)
- Beef tea, raw
- Boiled custard
- Boned garfish
- Brain cakes
- Brain cream
- Brains in potato cases
- Braised quail
- Bread and milk
- Bread jelly
- Bread sauce
- Bread soufflé
- Cake, tea
- Cakes, brain
- Calf's foot jelly
- Carrot salad
- Carrots, mashed
- Cauliflower soup
- Celery and walnut sandwiches
- Celery, stewed
- Cheese straws
- Cheese toast
- Chestnut force meat
- Chestnut sauce
- Chestnuts, curried
- Chicken, cold in white jelly
- Chicken cream
- Chicken croquettes
- Chicken cutlet
- Chicken, roast and bread sauce
- Chipped potatoes
- Chops, fricasseed
- Chops, grilled
- Cold meat and beetroot salad
- Custard shape
- Cutlets
- Date and almond sandwiches
- Egg, boiled
- Egg, croquette
- Egg, French method
- Egg, scrambled
- Eggnog
- Egg, poached
- Egg, steamed
- Fish toast
- Fish, to fry a fillet of
- Fricasseed brains
- Fricasseed chops
- Fricasseed or stewed oysters
- Fried brains

- Fried oysters
- Fried sweetbreads
- Fruits, to stewed
- Gem scones
- Grilled chops or steak
- Grilled steak and oysters
- Gruel
- Lemon or wine jelly
- Lemon sauce
- Lemon sponge
- Milk jelly
- Minced kidney
- Minced meat on toast
- Mock cream
- Mutton broth
- Oatmeal water
- Omelette, savoury
- Omelette, sweet soufflé
- Omelette, whitebait
- Orange soufflé
- Orange sponge
- Oyster cream sandwiches
- Oyster fritters
- Parsnip croquettes
- Pikelets
- Pineapple shape
- Potato chips
- Potato roses
- Prune shape
- Pumpkin scones
- Raw meat rissole
- Raw meat sandwiches
- Rice pudding without egg
- Rice, boiled
- Rice water
- Rissole
- Sago cream
- Sago custard
- Salmon cakes
- Salmon croquettes
- Savoury macaroni
- Scalloped oysters
- Scalloped salmon
- Scotch eggs
- Semolina soufflé
- Steamed whiting with oysters
- Stewed pigeon
- Stuffed cucumber
- Stuffed potatoes
- Sweetbreads, creamed
- Sweetbreads, fried
- Sweetbreads with sherry sauce
- Swiss roll
- Tea cake
- Tomato and celery salad
- Tomato and eggs
- Tomato jelly
- Tomato sandwiches
- Tomatoes and macaroni
- Tripe stewed in milk
- Whey
- Wine whey

The J. H. Redmond Cookery Book and Household Guide. (Redmond, 1912) [Hoyle 1136]
<u>Recipe</u> (p118)
- Beef tea (for invalids)

Lee's Priceless Recipes: The standard collection of famous formulas and simple methods (revised edition). (Oliver, 1912) [Not in Hoyle]

Recipes (pp171-172)
- Sago cream and extract of beef
- Tapioca and cod liver
- Burdete's restorative jelly
- Invalid's jelly
- Beef tea custard
- Beef jelly

The Liberals' Cookery Book: Being good and tried recipes contributed by ladies from all parts of South Australia. (Schlank, 1912) [Hoyle 1222]

Recipes (pp85-90)
- Barley water
- Beef tea (2 recipes)
- Brain cutlets
- Cornflour
- Eggs in milk
- Egg broth
- Eggnog
- Fish custard
- Baked fish
- Gruel
- Rabbit or chicken jelly
- Calf's foot jelly
- Oatmeal drink
- Rice soup
- Nourishing soup for invalids
- Marrow sandwiches
- Stewed sweetbreads
- Toast water

The Practical Australian Cookery: A collection of up-to-date tried recipes for domestic and general use (3rd edition). (Monro, 1912) [Hoyle 884]

Advice (pp143-144)

[General advice on invalid cookery, including]:

In preparing food for an invalid it must be borne in mind that the range of food is very limited, and that certain methods of cooking are quite inadmissible. Pork, and often veal, the richer kinds of fish and all kinds of pastry must be quite put aside. Dry frying is out of the question, and, generally speaking, baking also.

In an acute state of illness, food is scarcely required at all, milk being the only real food taken for days together. It is during recovery and the period of convalescence that the question of food must be carefully studied, and the right kind of food given of sufficient variety to stimulate the appetite without giving those kinds of foods which to an invalid would be indigestible.

Recipes (pp144-154)
- Beef tea (3 recipes)
- Raw beef tea
- Mutton broth (2 recipes)
- Chicken broth
- Beef tea custard
- Toast water
- Barley water (2 recipes)
- Lemonade
- Apple water
- Rice water
- Sago cream soup
- Stewed oysters
- Calf's foot jelly
- Beef jelly
- Milk jelly
- Grilled fish
- Chicken cutlet
- Chicken croquettes

- Chicken stewed in milk
- Egg flip
- Scalloped brains
- Brain cakes
- Fricassee brains
- Baked sweetbreads
- Stewed chop and rice
- Gruel
- Arrowroot or cornflour
- Semolina pudding
- Tapioca cream
- Sweet omelette
- Apple delight
- Light bread pudding
- Wine whey
- Egg jelly
- Bran tea
- Koumis [milk, honey and yeast]
- Rice cream soup
- Treacle posset
- Angel's food
- Peptonised beef tea
- Peptonised gruel
- Peptonised milk

1913 (4th edition) identical recipes
<u>Revised advice, including:</u>
In severe illnesses the patient is often not able to digest food of any kind without some assistance. This is owing to lack of digestive juices; the gastric or pancreatic juices are deficient, and this is sometimes a serious condition. But certain foods can be digested outside the body, and the patient may be tided over a critical period. Thus it is easy to make milk, beef tea, gruel etc. perfectly digestible. Any chemist will supply the materials of which there are several kinds. The foods may be peptonised by the aid of peptonising power or pancreatised by the assistance of some liquor pancreaticus.
1914 (5th edition) identical recipes in different order
1919 (6th edition revised and enlarged) identical recipes
1922 (7th edition revised and enlarged) identical recipes

1913?

The New Zealand Domestic Cookery Book (5th edition). (Harman & Gard'ner, 1913?) [Hoyle 618]
<u>Advice</u> (p226-227) General Rules for invalid cookery:
1. The cooking for the sick room must be of the best, still it should be as simple and unpretentious as possible.
2. Never warm anything up for a sick person except broths; make everything as needed.
3. Use no acids in jellies or drinks except lemon juice.
4. When milk is too heavy and causes indigestion, give half milk and half soda water.
5. Have all the broths etc quite free from fat, absorb it with blotting paper.
6. If a pudding is allowed, it must be light and digestible. Use no soda, acid or baking powder.
7. All meat, fish etc must be well but lightly cooked. Boiled, more digestible than cooked in any other way. Lightly grilled chops, juicy, but not raw in the middle.
8. Have everything plain, no seasonings except a little salt and pepper, if allowed; under-season everything, as more salt can be put in.
9. In infectious diseases burn all food that comes from a sick room.
10. Grapes should be skinned and the pips taken out. Give only the yellow pulp of oranges, carefully removing all white tough skin and pips.

<u>Recipes</u> (pp227-238)
- Beef tea
- Beef essence
- Mutton broth
- Meat tea
- Gravy soup
- Brain soup
- Chicken broth
- Gruel (2 recipes)
- Tapioca milk
- Biscuit milk
- Arrowroot
- Milk arrowroot
- Panada of bread and milk
- A nutritive toast
- Boiled flounder
- Steamed flounder
- Filleted flounder
- Chicken cream
- Chicken fillets
- Sweetbreads
- Sweetbreads fried
- Brain fried
- Scalloped brains
- Cream egg
- Eggs poached in gravy
- Scrambled eggs
- Poached egg
- Stewed tripe (2 recipes)
- Cutlets stewed in stock
- Stewed calf's feet
- Asparagus with cream
- Chicken jelly
- Meat jelly
- Calf's foot jelly
- Port wine or claret jelly
- Steamed cup custard
- Apple soufflé
- Fancy pudding
- Egg wine
- Nourishing drink
- Barley water (2 recipes)
- Milk lemonade
- Plain lemonade
- Oatmeal drink

1917 (6th edition) identical recipes

1913

The Australasian Cookery Book. (Anon, 1913) [Hoyle 54]
<u>Recipes</u> (various pages)
- Arrowroot (p36)
- Barley water (p41)
- Beef tea (p50)
- Currant water (p84)
- Gruel (p106)
- Invalid's jelly p113)

Australian Everyday Cookery: Hints on carving, preparing menus, laundry work and general housekeeping (6th edition). (A Professional Cook, 1913) [Hoyle 62]
<u>Advice</u> (pp312-313)
1. Food for invalids must be nourishing, digestible, well cooked and well served. Tender roast beef, nicely grilled steak or chops, chicken, boiled fish (if not too rich), oysters, lightly-cooked eggs, strong soups, beef tea, jellies and light puddings all form part of the diet in turn. Milk contains all the necessary food constituents and is therefore a perfect invalid's food if perfectly fresh; but it is sometimes found to be rather heavy if taken by itself. Half milk and half soda water, or milk with 1/8 part lime water may be recommended.

2. Use as little as possible of baking powders, powdered acids, and seasonings in invalid cookery. Lemon juice may be substituted for acids and flavourings were possible.
3. Do not serve warmed-up food to an invalid. Everything but broths should be freshly cooked.
4. Do not leave food of any sort in the sick-room. Be careful to exercise most scrupulous cleanliness. Serve everything in as dainty and appetising way as possible.

Recipes (pp313-318)
- Beef tea (2 recipes)
- Raw beef tea
- Beef essence (2 recipes)
- Oatmeal gruel
- Quaker oats with egg
- Linseed tea for colds
- Lime water
- Albumenised milk or water
- A cup of arrowroot
- Breadcrumb pudding
- Teacup custard pudding
- Baked milk for invalids
- To sterilise milk
- Rice water
- Boiled or baked flour
- Chicken broth
- Chicken cream
- Egg cream
- Peach foam
- Wine jelly
- Sherry and egg
- Dandelion tea
- Port wine negus
- Mulled wine
- Egg drink

1918 (10th edition) identical recipes
1925 (14th edition) identical recipes

Glennen's Cook Book: Written specially for those interested in preparing food for invalids, diabetics and infants (2nd edition). (Glennen, 1913) [Hoyle 574]

Advice (pp1-15)
[Includes general advice about feeding in disease, basic nutrition, and dietetic choices for obesity, tuberculosis, gout, gravel, scurvy, rickets, gastric ulcer, dyspepsia, diarrhoea, gall stones, biliousness, heart disease, flatulence, kidney diseases, neurasthenia, eczema and urticaria.]

Recipes (pp58-70)
- Lemon blancmange
- Milk pudding
- Minced chicken
- Apples and rice
- Apricot cream
- Apple trifle
- Baked orange pudding
- Basin of bread and Glaxo
- Cup of Glaxo
- Glaxo custard
- Glaxo jelly
- Pancakes
- Arrowroot charlotte
- Lemon blancmange
- Foam pudding
- Tapioca cream
- Homeopathic pudding
- Blancmange
- Summer pudding
- Rice cream
- Sponge pudding
- Golden fingers

- Valencia pudding
- Orange fool
- Bread and marmalade pudding
- Dutch apple cake
- Children's trifle
- Banana trifle
- Cream
- Banana and trifle custard
- Banana and orange pudding
- Bananas and bacon
- Apple and rice soufflé
- Baked apples for children
- Apple batter pudding
- Lemon sago
- Semolina pudding
- Glaxo jelly
- Gooseberry fool
- Ground rice custard
- Ground rice sauce
- Victoria pudding
- Yorkshire pudding
- Glaxo when travelling

What to Eat and When and How and Why: What to do by natural methods to recover health and prevent disease. (Huston, 1913) [Hoyle 675]
Recipes (pp73-79)
- Ambrosia
- Apple toast
- Banana toast
- Egg toast
- Fruit toast
- Fresh fruit toast
- Milk toast
- Tomato toast
- Zwieback
- Browned flour
- Cheese balls
- Cheese pudding
- Cheese sauce
- Cheese straws
- Creamed spinach
- Green corn fritters
- Italian rice
- Macaroni cheese
- Maize cheese
- Mock fish
- Nut roast
- Nut savoury
- Potato cheese
- Rissoles
- Savoury rice
- Semolina cheese

1914?

The Australian Home Cookery. (Anon, 1914?) [Hoyle 72]
Also published later as *The Tasmanian Home Cookery Book* (Anon, 192-?-c) [Hoyle 1291]
Advice (p169)
The best meat for invalids is mutton, beef and lamb, which is not too young. Sweetbreads ought to be given to invalids oftener than they are. Calves' feet and head, scalded and boiled until tender, are very nutritious, and chickens, pigeons and partridges are most inviting. All the above mentioned articles are easy of digestion, except perhaps beef, which requires to be gently stewed until tender, if for a delicate person just ordered to take meat after a serious illness.
Recipes (pp170-175)
- Arrowroot jelly
- Apple tea
- Barley gruel
- Barley water

- Beef tea
- Calf's foot jelly
- Caudle
- Chicken panada
- Chicken broth
- Cod liver with potatoes
- Rice and cod liver
- Cranberry jelly beverage
- Plain custard
- A refreshing drink in a fever
- Eggs
- Egg wine
- Fish (steamed)
- Fish (baked)
- Gloucester jelly
- Lemon water
- Meat (raw) – If the patient objects to the appearance of raw meat it should be made into sandwiches
- Meat (minced)
- Milk (baked)
- Milk porridge
- Milk porridge (French)
- Plain mutton broth
- Seasoned mutton broth
- Mutton broth with vermicelli
- Orange whey
- Orgeat
- Ground rice milk
- A saline draught
- Sago milk
- Sago
- Sippets, when stomach will not receive meat
- Shank jelly
- Toast water
- Tapioca jelly
- Veal broth (2 recipes)
- Veal tea
- Veal cutlets (steamed)

1914

The Commonsense Cookery Book (1st edition). (The New South Wales Public School Cookery Teachers' Association, 1914) [Hoyle 960]

Recipes (pp143-154)

- Albumen water
- Baked apple
- Apple delight
- Apple water
- Barley water (2 recipes)
- Beef tea
- Beef tea custard
- Bread and milk
- Light bread pudding
- Plain fricasseed brains
- Stewed chop and rice
- Chicken broth
- Cup of cornflour or arrowroot
- Steamed custard
- Egg flip
- Grilled fish
- Steamed fish
- Cup of gruel
- Junket
- Lemon drink
- Savoury omelette
- Sweet omelette
- Toast water

1919 (2nd new & revised edition) identical recipes
1925 (new and revised edition) identical recipes
1926 (new and revised edition) identical recipes

1931 (new and enlarged edition) (The N.S.W. Cookery Teachers Association, 1931) [Hoyle 970]

Recipes (pp164-177)
- Baked apple
- Apple delight
- Apple water
- Barley water (3 recipes)
- Beef tea (2 recipes)
- Beef tea custard
- Brain cakes
- Bread and milk
- Light bread pudding
- Fricasseed brains
- Stewed chop and rice
- Chicken broth
- Cup of cornflour or arrowroot
- Steamed custard
- Egg flip
- Grilled fish
- Steamed fish
- Cup of gruel
- Junket
- Lemon drink
- Savoury omelette
- Scalloped brains
- Sweet omelette
- Toast water
- Clear jelly
- Angel's food

1934 (new and enlarged edition) identical recipes to 1931
1937 (new and enlarged edition) identical recipes to 1931
1941 (new and enlarged edition) identical recipes to 1931
1944 (new and enlarged edition) identical recipes to 1931
1946 (new and enlarged edition) identical recipes to 1931
1963 identical recipes to 1931, plus 2 beef tea recipes

1970 (revised edition) (The New South Wales Public School Cookery Teachers' Association, 1970)

Same recipes plus a list of other suitable dishes:
- Tomato cream soup
- Fish cream
- Scalloped oysters
- Poached, steamed or scrambled egg
- Grilled chops, steak or cutlets
- Fricasseed lamb, chicken or rabbit
- Fricasseed tripe
- Apple snow
- Blancmange
- College pudding
- Baked custards
- Fruit flummery
- Lemon sago
- Stewed fruit
- Sweet poached eggs
- Sponge sandwich

1974 (metric edition) (The N.S.W. Public School Cookery Teachers' Association, 1974)

Recipes (pp213-226)
- Apple delight
- Baked apple
- Arrowroot or cornflour gruel
- Barley water
- Beef tea (2 recipes)
- Beef tea custard
- Brain cakes
- Fricasseed brains
- Scalloped brains
- Bread and milk
- Light bread pudding
- Chicken broth
- Stewed chops and rice
- Steamed custard
- Egg flip
- Gruel

- Junket
- Lemon drink
- Milk jelly
- Savoury omelette
- Sweet omelette

Plus additional dishes as in 1970 edition

1988 (revised edition) (Trustees of the NSW Cookery Teachers Scholarship Fund, 1988)

Advice (p250)

[Limited section on Special Diets says for The Convalescent]: Food selected should be easily digested because the digestive system is usually impaired by illness. The appetite needs to be stimulated by light and attractive meals served in small portion.

Recipes (p250)

"Children, the aged and convalescents could be served such dishes as the following" (with page numbers provided to recipes in the regular section of the book):

- Fruit juice
- Eggs cooked in shells
- Steamed egg
- Scrambled egg
- Poached egg
- Egg flip
- Rolled oats
- Broth
- Tomato cream soup
- Steamed fish
- Grilled fish
- Fish mould
- Lambs' brains
- Grilled chops or French cutlets
- Irish stew
- Fricasseed lamb, chicken or rabbit
- Creamed chicken
- Stewed chops and rice
- Vegetables – boiled, steamed baked
- Salads
- Baked cheese custard
- Cheese and vegetable bake
- Macaroni cheese
- Spaghetti bolognaise
- Savoury omelette
- Tuna and pumpkin
- Rissoles
- Bread and butter pudding
- Angel's food
- Blancmange
- Junket
- Stirred custard
- Arrowroot or cornflour
- Gruel
- Light bread pudding
- Milk jelly
- Apple snow
- Apple sponge
- Banana custard
- Fresh fruit salad
- Vanilla ice-cream
- Fruits
- Barley water
- Lemon drink
- Homemade yoghurt

2013 (Centenary edition) (Home Economics Institute of Australia (NSW Division), 2013)

No invalid cookery information

Everything a Lady Should Know: A book of everyday requirements comprising 1100 useful recipes (12th edition). (Anon, 1914) [Hoyle 495]
Recipes (pp104-108)
- Apple water
- Barley cream
- Barley water
- Beef tea (3 recipes)
- A strong broth
- Chicken broth
- Coffee milk
- Savoury custard
- Egg on toast
- Flaxseed tea (an excellent drink in fever accompanied by a cough)
- Flaxseed lemonade
- Gruel (3 recipes_
- Hot lemonade
- Milk (hot)
- Mutton broth
- Onion gruel
- Orange jelly
- Rice jelly
- Rice water
- Soothing nourishment in consumption
- Toast
- Toast water (2 recipes)
- Toast sandwiches for invalid

1915? (14th edition) identical recipes
1924 (26th edition) identical recipes

Sylvia's Cookery Book. (Farrell, 1914) [Hoyle 501]
Recipes (pp95-96)
- Cup custard
- Beef tea custard
- Beef tea
- Raw beef tea
- Knuckle broth
- Barley water
- Sherry whey
- Baked apples
- Nourishing blancmange
- Steamed chicken
- Calf's foot milk jelly
- Chicken broth
- Rice milk
- Chicken in jelly
- Baked apple and sago
- Stewed chicken in milk

1915

"Everylady's" Cook Book: Containing over 600 recipes tested and proved good (5th edition). (White, 1915) [Hoyle 492]
[Note: not the same as *Everylady's Cook-Book* (Drake, 1924)]
Advice (p93)
[General advice on invalid cookery]

Recipes (pp94-100)
- Strengthening broth
- Mutton broth
- Beef tea
- Beef tea jelly
- Oysters
- Fried oysters
- Pigs in blankets
- Stewed sheep trotters
- Ragout of sweetbreads
- Brain cutlets

- Stewed rabbit
- Tripe
- Tripe cutlets
- To poach an egg
- Steamed eggs
- Omelette
- Spatchcock
- To grill a joint of chicken
- Chicken custard
- Chicken panada
- Peach foam
- Lemon sponge
- Caramel cream
- Arrowroot
- Tapioca cream
- Junket
- Boiled custard
- Lemon jelly
- Calf's foot jelly
- Barley water
- To prepare lime water
- Toast water
- Lemonade
- Albumenised milk
- Refreshing drink for the sick (blackcurrant jam and hot water)

The Hamilton Cookery Book of Tried Recipes (2nd edition). (Simpson & Gummov, 1915) [Hoyle 1241]

Recipes (pp1-3)

- Invalid's soup
- Beef tea
- Raw beef tea
- Milk soup
- White soup
- Rice soup
- Cold apple soup

Housekeeping for Two or More: Casserole and general cookery (5th edition). (Winning, 1915) [Hoyle 1387]

Recipes (pp46-47)

- Grilled mince on toast
- Raw beef sandwiches
- Meat juice
- Rum and milk
- Barley water
- Egg brandy

The Red Cross Cookery Book: 250 recipes. (Lowe, 1915) [Hoyle 779]

Recipes (pp49-50).

Section on "To make the best use of a fowl for an invalid" contains directions to use one bird to make:

- Steamed chicken
- Chicken broth
- Chicken gravy
- Moulded minced chicken
- Chicken custard
- Chicken fricassee with oysters

Between 1915 and 1922

Swinburne Technical College Glenferrie: Student's text book for home cookery. (Drake, Between 1915 and 1922) [Hoyle 426]

Recipes (various pages)
- Beef tea (2 recipes) (p85)
- Beef tea raw (p85)
- Barley water (p86)
- Boiled fish (p26)
- Brains and bacon (p84)
- Chicken croquettes (p79)
- Charlotte Russe (p18)
- Clear barley water (p89)
- Chicken broth (p87)
- Coffee (p34)
- Dandy custard (p10)
- Fried fish (p26)
- Grills (p40)
- Grilled fish (p85)
- Junket (p34)
- Lemon sauce for fish (p90)
- Lemonade (p87)
- Mock whitebait (p5)
- Omelettes (p54)
- Steamed egg (p33)
- Sago cream soup (p22)
- Scalloped oysters (p77)
- Scrambled egg (p73)
- Siberian cream (p89)
- Sweetbreads and bacon (p81)
- Toast water (p86)
- Various meals for an invalid from one chicken (p87)

1916

The Australian Household Guide. (Hackett, 1916) [Hoyle 752]

Advice (pp576-577)

After an illness, when the patient has been kept solely on milk diet, the doctor frequently orders a change to light and nourishing food. Do not imagine this means only such things as beef tea, jelly and fruit. These, though refreshing and stimulating to a certain degree, are not themselves very nourishing foods and one cannot live very long upon stimulants alone.

Solid foods may certainly be given in an easily digested form, and a patient upon a "light" diet should always have plenty of eggs and milk. All kinds of puddings may be given, but it is always advisable to vary these, as invalids, especially children, are apt to take a violent dislike to milk preparations of any description.

Milk jelly or blancmange is generally liked, and is both nourishing and refreshing, but it is always advisable to vary the monotony by flavouring sometimes with lemon, vanilla, almond, or perhaps a little blackcurrant jelly. Junket too is an excellent food, especially when served with flavoured and whipped cream.

Savoury custards make a welcome change from ordinary sweet custard.

Another way in which milk can be disguised is by adding it to vegetables such as onion, carrot, turnip, celery cut into very small pieces to form a soup.

White meats such as chicken, rabbit and game may be given if prepared in an appetising and nourishing way, but only fish such as flounder, whiting or garfish are allowed.

Eggs should be served in milk puddings, or beaten in milk, so that they can be easily digested.

Recipes (pp575-580)
- Chicken broth
- Chicken for invalids
- To boil a fowl for invalids
- Milk jelly (2 recipes)
- Chicken jelly (3 recipes)
- Chicken for invalids
- Beef tea pudding
- Beef tea custard
- Fricassee of tripe
- Invalid's beef pudding
- Chicken custard
- Invalid's pudding
- Meat jelly

1940 Lady Hackett's Household Guide. (Murphy, 1940) [Hoyle 753]
Identical text

Common-Sense Hints on Plain Cookery: A companion to the Commonsense Cookery Book. (The Cookery Teachers' Association of New South Wales, 1916) [Not in Hoyle]
Advice (pp94-95)
22 General Rules, including:
1. Obtain a diet list from the doctor in attendance and obey his orders implicitly.
2. Foods for the sick should be nourishing, light, tempting and easily digested.
3. Do not over-sweeten or over-flavour food, as the palate of the patient is very sensitive.
4. Remove every particle of fat from broths, soups, or beef tea with white kitchen paper or blotting paper.
5. Do not give any kind of alcoholic beverages, unless by the doctor's orders.
6. Beverages for the sick may be broadly divided into three classes:
   - Those which are nourishing, as milk, egg flip, barley water, cocoa, milk tea, gruel
   - Those given medicinally, as rice water, apple water, toast water
   - Those give to quench the thirst, as invalid's lemonade
7. Beef tea is more stimulating than nourishing; if carefully made it is appetising and gives variety to the diet.
8. Jelly contains very little nourishment but is useful as a means of introducing more valuable materials in an agreeable form, as milk, fruit juice, eggs, wine etc. Calves' feet jelly is the best foundation, next comes isinglass.
9. Gruel is very nourishing and heat producing. It should be made with all milk and the best Scottish oatmeal. As it excites perspiration it should always be given to the patient in bed. Gruel should be thin enough to drink.
10. Milk tea is stimulating and nourishing and is preferable to tea made with water.
11. Junket is very easily digested.
12. Fish is the lightest form of solid food and is much used in invalid dietary. Delicately-flavoured, white-fleshed fish are best, as whiting, bream, garfish etc.
13. Brains are light and easily digested.
14. Oysters are most easily digested when served raw.
15. Arrowroot, cornflour, Maizena and gelatine are not nourishing themselves but they are useful as a means to vary the ways in which eggs, milk, wine etc may be given. Gelatine helps repair the waste tissue, starchy foods give heat.

Recipes (p98)
Suitable dishes for convalescents (readers are referred to recipes in Common-Sense Cookery Book):

- Broths (mutton, veal, chicken and rabbit)
- White soups (oyster, fish, white vegetables)
- Beef tea (good, and beef tea custard)
- Fish (steamed, grilled or boiled)
- Brains
- Sweetbreads
- Tripe
- Chicken
- Rabbit
- Eggs (poached or lightly boiled)
- Oysters
- Egg flip
- Junket
- Bread and milk
- Wheatmeal porridge
- Gruel
- Steamed custard
- Milk puddings
- Blancmange
- Milk jelly
- Wine jelly
- Baked apple
- Cocoa
- Brown bread and butter
- Toast
- Biscuits
- Sponge cake
- Rusks
- Hot or cold milk
- Milk tea

1919 (2nd edition) identical information about invalid cookery

The Milky Way Housewife's Book: Containing one hundred recipes. (Nestlé, 1916) [Hoyle 941]

Recipes [all made with Nestle's condensed milk]
- Invalid's blancmange (p39)
- Invalid's pudding (p67)

1917 edition identical recipes

Our Cookery Book (1st edition). (Pell, 1916) [Hoyle 1034]

Advice (pp175-176)
The following are the diets generally ordered:
  Ordinary or Full Diet – Consists of meat, bread, with vegetables in variety
  Low Diet – Liquids such as teas, weak broth, barley water, thin gruel, arrowroot
  Milk Diet – Milk, arrowroot, sago, tapioca, rice, bread
  Vegetable Diet – Meat is dispensed with, fish and fowl being, however, generally allowed occasionally
  Meat Diet – Meat, cheese, eggs, milk, beef tea, broth, etc.

Recipes (pp176-184)
- Beef tea (2 recipes)
- Invalid gruel
- Toast water
- Cup custard
- Thick barley water
- Arrowroot
- Invalid chop
- Treacle posset

- Chicken broth
- Various meals for invalid from one chicken
- Sweet omelette
- Savoury omelette
- Light bread pudding
- Mutton broth
- Albumen water
- Apple water
- Beef tea custard
- Egg flip
- Stewed chop and rice
- Fricasseed brains
- Tapioca cream

1942 (18th edition) identical recipes
1949 (22nd edition) identical recipes
1950 (24th edition) identical recipes

The YLG Cookery Book. (Members of the Young Ladies' Guild, 1916) [Not in Hoyle]
Recipes (pp7-11)
- Stewed chop and rice
- Beef juice
- Arrowroot jelly
- Milk jelly
- Barley water
- Toast water
- Steamed fish
- Baked custard
- Steamed fish with sauce
- Beef jelly
- Cup custard
- Egg jelly
- Orange jelly recipe for invalids
- An excellent gruel for invalids
- Baked fish
- Apple delight
- Chicken cream
- Steamed eggs

1917

Barossa Cookery Book: 400 tried recipes. (Anon, 1917a) [Hoyle 106]
No invalid cookery recipes

1933 (3rd edition) The Barossa Cookery Book: 1000 selected recipes. (Anon, 1933) [Hoyle 108]
Recipes (p154)
- Barley water (2 recipes)
- Cup custard for invalids
- Eggnog
- Oatmeal gruel
- Raw beef tea
- White of egg and water

193-? (5th edition) identical recipes
193-? (6th edition) identical recipes
1946 (10th edition) identical recipes
195-? (17th edition) identical recipes
195-? (20th edition) identical recipes
19?? (25th edition) identical recipes
19?? (26th edition) identical recipes
197-? (30th edition) identical recipes
197? (31st edition) identical recipes
1992 (31st edition) identical recipes

Invalid Cookery Class Recipes: As taught in the kitchen of the Metropolitan Gas Company, Melbourne. (Ross, 1917) [Hoyle 1164]

Recipes (pp9-51)

- Beef tea (2 recipes)
- Raw beef tea
- Beef juice
- Beef-tea jelly
- Spring soup maigre
- Stock
- Barley water (2 recipes)
- Mutton broth
- Mutton tea
- Chicken broth
- Chicken arrowroot
- Rice milk soup
- Pulled bread
- Rice water (2 recipes)
- Bran tea
- Toast water
- Milk and soda water
- White wine whey
- Albumin water
- Albuminised milk
- Lemonade
- Apple tea
- Milk and suet
- Barley jelly or gruel
- Groat and oatmeal gruel
- Milk posset
- Green peas boiled
- Boiled flour
- Arrowroot pudding
- Baked custard pudding
- Steamed custard pudding
- Tapioca pudding
- Egg jellies
- Lemon sponge
- Rice and sago pudding
- Little orange soufflés
- Blancmange
- Stewed fruit
- Baked apples
- Syrup compotes and stewed fruit
- Soufflé pudding
- Wine jelly
- Custard
- Egg flip
- Coffee jelly
- Claret jelly
- Egg brandy (2 recipes)
- Tripe
- Grilled chicken
- To blanch onion
- Chicken custard (2 recipes)
- Grilled mutton chop
- Braised sweetbread
- To blanch sweetbread
- Sheep's brains
- Brain fritters
- Croquettes of chicken
- Brown sauce
- Mince beef
- Stewed rabbit
- Beef cakes
- Oysters
- Scalloped oysters (2 recipes)
- To blanch oysters
- Oysters on toast
- White sauce
- Fillets of whiting
- Fish cakes
- Grilled whiting, sole or flounder
- Fried whiting
- Boiled eggs
- Steamed eggs
- Omelette
- Poached eggs
- Scrambled eggs
- To cook bacon
- Sandwich cake
- Scones
- Boiled or steamed potatoes
- Oatmeal porridge

- Roast fowl
- Boiled fowl
- Bread sauce
- Oatmeal tea
- Blackcurrant water
- Peptonised milk
- Peptonised milk gruel
- Apple water
- Thickened milk
- Treacle posset
- Barley water

The Southern Cross Domestic Science: Containing three year courses in cookery, housewifery & laundry work - for schools. (Anon, 1917b) [Hoyle 1261]

Advice (pp 68-69)
Rules for invalid cookery:
1. The food should be simple and not highly seasoned.
2. Serve the food punctually, daintily, a little at a time and often.
3. All hot dishes should be really hot and cold dishes quite cold.
4. Try to vary the food as much as possible, letting each dish come as a surprise.
5. Do not prepare food in the sick room, or leave uneaten food there.
6. Do not worry the patient to eat, but always have something in readiness such as soup, jelly, or a cooling drink if asked for.
7. The best and freshest ingredients only must be used.
8. All utensils etc must be spotlessly clean.
9. If pudding is allowed, use no soda, acid or baking powder.

Suitable food for invalids (p69)

Mutton is more easily digested than beef though slightly less nourishing. Sweetbreads and brains are very suitable. Poultry and game are tender, nourishing, and easily digested. Fish is a valuable food. White fish such as sole or flounder should be selected, as the flesh is quite free from fat. Oily fish, though nourishing, is not so digestible. Oysters are the only shell-fish allowable, and these eaten raw are most nourishing and digestible.

Milk, being the only perfect food in liquid form, is of great value. An addition of barley or soda water will in some cases render milk more digestible. Cream is nourishing and is easily made into appetising dishes.

Eggs are most digestible eaten raw or very lightly cooked; lightly cooked albumen contains much nourishment.

Soups, broths, and beef tea if well made possess valuable qualities in a very digestible form.

Coffee and tea contain very little nourishment, but have a stimulating effect on the nervous system, Cocoa is more of a food than a beverage, and contains considerable nourishment.

Green vegetables are wholesome if well cooked, especially spinach. Fruit is wholesome and refreshing. Care should be taken that it is ripe and in good condition.

Cooling drinks are toast water, barley water, milk and soda water, and lemon juice and water.

Recipes (pp67&70)
- Gruel
- Steamed fish
- Baked custard
- Beef tea
- Sago custard
- Stewed prunes or figs
- Baked apples

The War Chest Cookery Book. (The War Chest Fund, 1917) [Hoyle 60]
Recipes (pp113-125)

- Beef tea
- Mutton broth
- Celery soup
- Barley water
- Egg flip
- White of egg
- Gruel
- White sauce
- Baked fish
- Scalloped fish
- Fried fish
- Steamed whiting
- Fried brains
- Scalloped brains
- Stewed chicken
- Baked potatoes
- Savoury custard
- Baked chops
- Batter pudding
- Baked apple
- Boiled custard
- Steamed custard
- Stewed fruit
- Cup of arrowroot or cornflour
- Cup of sago
- Junket
- Lemon pudding
- Sponge sandwich
- Sponge pudding
- Plain or sultana cake
- Tapioca custard

1919

The Union Jack Cookery Book & Home Companion. (Union Jack, 1919) [Hoyle 1312]
Recipes (pp126-127)

- Oatmeal gruel
- Milk and rice soup
- Beef tea
- Beef essence
- Bovril and milk jelly
- Steamed fish puddings
- Chicken broth
- Stewed chop and rice
- Milk jelly
- Biscuit posset
- Honey mould
- Invalid drinks
- Albumen water
- Apple water

1920-1929

Dainty Dishes: A book of selected recipes by Nestlé's. (Nestlé, 192-?)

The Colonial Mutual Life Cookery Book (Colonial Mutual Life Assurance Society, 1924)

192-?

The Australia Recipe Book. (Matheson, 192-?) [Hoyle 817]
Recipes (p57)
- Toast water
- Whey
- White egg flip
- Hot drink for a cold [blackcurrant jam or jelly, sugar and water]
- Ginger syrup
- Elderberry syrup
- Barley water
- Welsh nectar

"Central" Cookery Book (1st edition). (Irvine, 192-?) [Hoyle 679]
Advice (p23)
[Invalid Cookery information, including]:
Beverages:
1. Nourishing as milk, barley water
2. Medicinal, as rice water, toast water
3. Thirst-quenching, as lemonade

Diets:
1. Ordinary or full diet – meat, vegetables and pudding
2. Low diet – liquids such as beef tea
3. Milk diet – milk, sago, rice etc
4. Vegetable diet – only white meats and vegetables allowed
5. Meat diet – only meat dishes, and cheese, eggs, broths etc are allowed

1935-39 (3rd edition) (Irvine, Between 1935 and 1939) [Hoyle 680]
Recipes (pp129-132)
- Beef tea (2 recipes)
- Beef tea (raw)
- Gruel
- Milk arrowroot
- Barley water
- Lemonade
- Steamed egg
- Steamed custard
- Egg flip
- Fricassee brains
- Chicken broth
- Gelatine blancmange
- White wine whey
- Lemon sponge

1940-50? (9th edition revised) identical to 3rd edition plus:
- Rusks
- Bread sticks

1976 (revised metric edition) identical to the 9th edition
1991 (16th edition) No invalid diet recipes
1992 (17th edition) No invalid diet recipes

Cookery Book Mainly for Nurses and Bachelor Girls (4th edition). (Shepherd, 192-?) [Hoyle 1237]
[Shepherd was teacher of invalid cookery at Royal Women's Hospital in Sydney and many others]
Recipes (various pages)
- Albumen water (p103)
- Albumenised sherry (p101)

- Apple water (p99)
- Beef tea (2 recipes) (p4)
- Beef tea, raw (p4)
- Benger's food (p64)
- Blancmange (p56)
- Brain cakes (p25)
- Brain fricassee (p24)
- Brains, scalloped (p25)
- Chicken broth (p9)
- Junket (p25)
- Lemon sago (p58)
- Lime water (p100)
- Liver cocktail (p27)
- Liver soup (p10)
- Liver soup, creamed (p10)
- Milk jelly (p53)
- Mutton broth (p8)
- Oysters mornay (p13)
- Panada (p95)
- Peptonised foods (p126)
- Prune sago (p58)
- Rice water (p100)
- Sago custard (p59)
- Spanish cream (p48)
- Sweetbreads, creamed (p22)
- Sweetbreads, scalloped (p22)
- Tripe, creamed (p23)
- Toast water (p101)
- Wine whey (p102)

Cookery Book: Tried and tested recipes. (The Women's Guild of St Peter's Church of England Croydon, 192-?) [Hoyle 227]
Recipe (p23)
- A wonderfully strengthening tonic (Specially good for weak chests and nerves and to build one up after an illness) [eggs, lemon, olive oil, honey and rum]

Dainty Dishes: A book of selected recipes by Nestlé's. (Nestlé, 192-?) [Hoyle 935]
Recipes (p23)
- Biscuits or rusks with Lactogen
- Cereal puddings with Lactogen
- Baked custard
- Ground rice with Lactogen

Home Cookery and Jewish Recipes. (Marks, 192-?) [Hoyle 807]
Recipes (pp66-67)
- Toast water
- Hot drink for a cold
- Ginger syrup
- Home brewed beer
- Elderberry syrup
- Barley water
- Chili punch
- Lemon syrup
- Welsh nectar
- Whey
- White egg flip

The Householder's Friend. (Naylor, 192-?) [Hoyle 932]
Recipes (pp34-36)
- White of egg and milk
- Steamed egg
- Barley water
- Cup custard
- Oatmeal gruel
- Rice gruel

- Wheatmeal gruel
- Brains
- Invalid chop
- Blackcurrant tea (for a persistent cough)

The Ladies Delight Recipe Book. (Anon, 192-?-a) [Hoyle 751]

Recipes (p25)
- Nutritious beef tea
- Tapioca jelly
- Milk jelly

The Pinnaroo Soldiers' Memorial Cookery Book. (Anon, 192-?-b) [Hoyle 1054]

Advice (p 52) including:

Food that cannot be easily digested is of no use and the taking of it by the patient can be productive of nothing but discomfort and loss of future appetite.

Gelatine and starchy foods, except as a way of conveying the wine or milk or eggs, contain very little nourishment.

Serving small quantities and in a dainty manner will often induce an appetite.

Recipes (pp52-55)
- Beef tea
- Chicken broth for invalids
- Apple water (invalid)
- Barley water (2 recipes)
- Boiled milk (invalid)
- Hot drink for a cold (invalid)
- Albumen water
- Beef tea custard
- Milk for invalids
- Rabbit or chicken jelly
- Toast water
- White egg flip
- Linseed tea (for coughs)

Red Cross Emergency Cookery Book. (Newman, 192-?) [Not in Hoyle]

Advice (pp31-63)

[12 lectures plus extensive section on Invalid Cookery]

Recipes (pp34-63)
- Fish custard
- Fish stewed in milk
- Fish soufflé baked
- Fricassee of oysters
- Steamed fish
- A restorative soup
- Mutton broth
- Chicken broth
- Celery or rice soup
- Cream of barley
- Sago cream soup
- Stewed oxtail soup
- Mutton quenelles
- Fricasseed brains
- Chicken and macaroni timbales
- Creamed liver
- Creamed chicken
- Beef creams
- Boiled pigeon
- Tripe and onions

- Sweet omelette
- Spanish cream
- Queen pudding
- Pineapple and cornflour meringue
- Meringued peaches
- Lemon sponge
- Junket
- Hasty pudding
- Custard pie
- Caramel rice pudding
- Apple cream
- A delicate bread pudding
- Apple and tapioca pudding
- Banana cream
- Baked apple custard
- Castle puddings
- Caramel custard
- Stewed fruits
- Snow capped apples
- Tapioca cream
- Thin custard
- Buttered apples
- Root vegetables
- Green vegetables
- Mashed potatoes
- Toast water
- Treacle posset (for a cold)
- Rum and milk
- Rice water
- Milk gruel
- Lemonade
- Egg and rum
- Egg flip
- Albuminised milk or water
- Cocoa
- Coffee
- Coffee or tea with egg
- Brandy and egg mixture
- Bran tea (a remedy for hoarseness)
- Blackcurrant drink
- Apple water
- Linseed tea
- Egg jelly
- Milk jelly
- Prune soufflé
- Wine jelly
- Parsley sauce
- Jam sauce

Simple Cookery for the People: Easy and economical dishes. (Senn, 192-?) [Hoyle 1229]
<u>Recipes</u> (pp53-56)
- Arrowroot cup
- Arrowroot pudding
- Barley water (2 recipes)
- Beef tea
- Beef tea custard
- Blackcurrant tea
- Custard pudding
- Egg flip
- Gruel
- Junket
- Lemonade, home-made
- Linseed tea
- Suet and milk

St Paul's Cookery Book. Miss P. De Boos (De Boos, 192-?) [Hoyle 370]
<u>Recipe</u> (no page numbers)
- A nourishing dish for invalids

1920

The Armidale Red Cross Cookery Book of Tested Recipes (2nd edition). (Armidale Branch Red Cross Society, 1920) [Hoyle 1127]

Recipes (pp77-79)
- Stewed chop
- Invalid pudding
- Cup custard
- A nourishing drink for invalids
- Egg flip
- Jelly water
- Barley water
- Arrowroot
- Gruel

Aunt Susan's Recipes. (Susan, 1920) [Hoyle 53]

Recipes (pp59-61)
- Toast water
- Mutton broth
- Light bread pudding
- Baked sweetbreads
- Tapioca cream
- Apple delight
- Egg flip
- Gruel
- Grilled fish
- Arrowroot or cornflour

1921

PWMU Cookery Book of Victoria (4th edition).
(The Presbyterian Women's Missionary Union of Victoria, 1921) [Hoyle 1097]

Advice (pp167-168) [General hints for the nurse and rule for sickroom cookery, including]:
Beef tea is valuable as a stimulant but does not contain much nourishment.

Eggs are of value sometimes, three or four being given to a patient in one day.

Arrowroot is palatable and non-irritating. It is simply a starch food and does not contain much nourishment. It is more nourishing when made with milk.

Milk is a valuable food, but is found difficult to digest by some patients, in which case it should be diluted or specially prepared, such as peptonised milk.

Recipes (pp169-173)
- Apple, stewed
- Apple water
- Apple soufflé
- Arrowroot made with milk
- Batter pudding
- Barley custard pudding
- Bovril, home-made
- Beef tea (2 recipes)
- Beef tea custard
- Calf's foot broth
- Chop, steamed
- Chicken for invalids
- Chicken broth
- Grilled chicken
- Steamed chicken
- Roast chicken
- Chicken ramekins
- Coddled egg
- Cutlet, grilled
- Fish eggs
- Fish, steamed
- Fish pudding
- Tapioca cream soup

Beverages (pp174-177)
- Barley water (2 recipes)
- Blackcurrant vinegar
- Boston cream
- Cereal coffee
- Coffee
- Chili beer
- Ginger beer
- Hop beer
- Lemonade
- Lemon syrup
- Lemon whey
- Linseed tea
- O.T. [drink of sugar, chillies, cloves, cayenne pepper and lemon]
- Raspberry vinegar
- Rice water

1927 (8th edition) identical to 4th edition

1936 The New PWMU Cookery Book. (Campbell, 1936) [Hoyle 1099]

Recipes (pp192-197)
- Beef tea
- Bovril and beaten egg
- Chicken broth
- Chicken essence
- Chicken custard
- Rabbit patties
- Raw beef sandwiches
- Steamed chicken
- Steamed fish soufflé
- Steamed whiting
- Stewed rabbit
- Omelette
- Arrowroot soufflé
- Calf's foot jelly
- Custard mould
- Egg jelly
- Arrowroot
- Arrowroot and blackcurrant tea
- Barley water
- Blackcurrant tea
- Egg flip
- Gruel

1941 identical recipes to 1936 edition
1948 identical recipes to 1936 edition
1973 PWMU Cookery Book. (Howat & Miersch, 1973)
Revised metric edition – no invalid diet information

Your Own Stores Book of Cookery.
(Eudunda Farmers' Co-operative Society Ltd, 1921) [Hoyle 487]

Recipes (pp78-80)
- Beef tea
- Beef tea jelly
- Beef tea custard
- Mutton broth (is given to patients suffering from inflammatory disorders)
- Invalid broth
- Celery cream soup
- Chicken broth

1922

Invalid Cookery: Recipes used in nurses' cookery classes and approved by the ATNA. (Fowler, 1922) [Hoyle 543]

Advice (pp7-9)

[General introductory advice on invalid cookery is very similar to that in the author's earlier book (Fowler, 1910), but also includes]:

Gelatine and starchy foods except as a means of conveying wine or milk or eggs contain very little nourishment. Tender roast beef, nicely-grilled steak or chops, chicken, boiled fish (if not too rich), oysters, lightly-cooked eggs, strong soups, beef tea, jellies, and light puddings, may all form part of the diet in turn.

Milk contains all the necessary food constituents, and is therefore the perfect invalid's food, but it is sometimes found to be rather heavy if taken by itself. Half milk and half soda water, or milk with about one-eighth part lime water may then be recommended.

Use as little as possible of baking powders, powdered acids and seasoning for Invalid Cookery.

The chief aim of a good nurse is to provide her patient with good, nourishing and easily-digested food.

Recipes (pp14-62)

- Lemonade
- Orangeade
- Toast water
- Barley water (2 recipes)
- Apple water
- Cream of tartar
- Egg flip
- Egg and brandy milk
- Milk and rum
- White wine whey
- Arrowroot water
- Albuminised milk or water
- Gruel
- Steamed custard
- Baked custard
- Boiled custard
- Sago or tapioca cream
- Rice custard
- Sweet omelette
- Savoury omelette
- Poached egg
- Junket
- Steamed fish
- White sauce
- Baked whiting
- Baked apples
- Canary pudding
- White sweet sauce
- Caramel pudding
- Queen pudding
- Chicken broth
- Boiled fowl
- Parsley sauce
- Baked fowl
- Beans
- Peas
- Bread sauce
- Brown gravy
- Egg snow
- Plain cornflour mould
- Siberian cream
- Lemon sponge
- Beef tea (2 recipes)
- Raw beef tea
- Mutton broth
- Sago cream soup
- Brains in batter
- Sweetbreads
- Mashed potatoes

The "Lifeguard" Cookery Book. (Drake, 1922) [Hoyle 436]
["Lifeguard" was a brand of condensed milk]
Advice (pp60-61)
When the crisis is past, the system needs nothing but complete nutrition – the appetite may be clamorous, or fickle, or altogether wanting. It is then the time to test the tact, skill and patience of the nurse and cook (often combined of necessity in the same person) – the mother.

Avoid salted meat, pork, veal, oily fish, duck and geese, and remember that mutton is slightly less nourishing than beef, but it is more easily digested, so more suited to convalescents and children.

A few rules:
1. Give small quantities at short intervals.
2. Try to anticipate the patient's wants, and recollect that thirst is nearly always present on waking; therefore have a drink ready, so that the patient will not need to ask for it, nor wait while it is obtained.
3. Never ask invalids what they would like to eat, unless you have noticed their enjoyment of a certain dish, then it may be suggested to them.
4. Avoid all risk of the smell of cooking entering the sick room.
5. Serve rather less, than more, than the patient will probably require. Do not judge his appetite by your own, and overload the plate, or offer an over-large bowl of soup. He may become filled with loathing or nausea, and probably refuse to partake of it at all, which disappoints the nurse, and is bad for the patient.
6. A small whole jelly, or pudding, or custard, is much preferable to serving from a large one. It is also more economical. Food, especially that suitable for invalids, is expensive, and though we do not grudge the cost, it is wasteful to cook too much.
7. When the meal is over, remove every trace of it from the sick-room, but it is quite admissible to keep in the room choice fruit or delicacies – which have been sent to the patient by friends – just long enough to gratify the eye of the patient.

Recipe (p61)
- Gruel

Between 1923 and 1929

Dainty Dishes for Children, Invalids and Convalescents (1st edition).
(Drake & Giles, Between 1923 and 1929) [Hoyle 416]
[A textbook for Nurses Cookery Certificate training]
Advice (pp1-6)
[Much general advice on diets for invalids, including about the kinds of foods best suited to invalids, convalescents and children, including]:
Mutton is slightly less nourishing than beef but is more easily digested.

Salted meat, pork and veal are difficult to digest. Not permissible

Bacon is a popular and wholesome form of fat. It should be toasted, grilled or well boiled, so do not use very lean bacon.

Poultry and game are tender, tempting, nourishing, and very easily digested. Do not give duck or goose, unless specifically ordered. They are too rich.

Fish is a valuable food. Choose the white fleshed varieties, because more of the oil is stored in the liver of these fish, leaving an entire absence of fat in the flesh. Oily fish (though nourishing) often upsets the digestion.

Oysters when eaten raw are nourishing and digestible. They can often be retained on the stomach when other foods cause vomiting.

Soup is useful in our diet, apart from the actual nourishment it contains. It warms the stomach and prepares it to assimilate the heavier foods which follow. A plate of good soup will revive a tired person sooner than a meal of more solid food, though the effect is, of course, not so long lasting.

Recipes (pp7-36)
- Albumen water
- Apple cream
- Asparagus
- Baked onions in milk
- Barley water
- Beef tea (2 recipes)
- Beef tea raw
- Blancmange
- Boiled fowl and egg sauce
- Boiled mutton
- Brains and bacon
- Brains on toast
- Braised sweetbreads
- Bread sauce
- Bread and butter pudding
- Brussels spouts
- Caramel custard
- Cauliflower
- Chicken broth
- Chops, steamed
- Chops, stewed
- Coconut pudding
- Cocoa
- Coffee
- College pudding
- Compote of apples
- Custard baked
- Custard boiled
- Cup custard
- Devon pudding
- Date pudding
- Eggs boiled
- Eggs buttered
- Eggs steamed
- Eggs scrambled
- Fish baked
- Fish boiled
- Fish fried fillets
- Fish grilled
- Fish steamed
- Green peas
- Grilled chops or steak
- Gruel
- Jelly fruit
- Jelly lemon egg
- Jellied milk
- Jelly nourishing
- Lemonade
- Lemon sauce
- Macaroni pudding
- Marrow
- Marrow sandwiches
- Meat stock
- Milk puddings
- Mock whitebait
- Mutton broth
- Mutton or lamb cutlets
- Omelette savoury
- Omelette sweet
- Oyster sandwiches
- Oysters scalloped
- Oyster soup
- Porridge
- Potatoes creamed

- Potatoes mashed
- Potatoes new
- Potatoes old
- Raw beef rolls
- Rice pudding
- Roast fowl
- Roast mutton, lamb, beef, pork
- Sago pudding
- Sago cream soup
- Salads
- Sandwiches
- Sauces
- Soups
- Spatchcock
- Spinach
- Steamed puddings
- Tapioca pudding
- Toast water
- Tomato soup
- Trifle fruit
- Tripe stewed
- Various meals for an invalid from one chicken
- Veal forcemeat
- Viennoise pudding
- White sauce
- Wholemeal bread

1939 (4th edition) (Drake & Giles, 1939) [Not in Hoyle]
Recipes same as 1st edition, plus
- Iced beef tea
- Chicken essence
- A delicious fish soup
- Boiled bream, Murray cod etc
- Mock whitebait
- Liver puree
- General rules for cooking vegetables
- Flummery
- Baked orange or lemon pudding
- Butterscotch pudding
- Cream of rice
- Caramel puffs
- Wine jelly
- Wine and whey jelly
- Fruit or wine jelly
- Fruit trifle
- Chocolate pudding

1923

Excell Cook Book: for the Junior Red Cross. (Aronson, 1923) [Hoyle 50]
Recipes (pp137-138)
- Invalid's boiled custard
- Apple tea
- Groat's gruel
- Egg soup
- Egg fillip (this makes an excellent stimulant and restorative drink) [egg, brandy or rum and sugar]

Mrs. Beeton's All-About Cookery with over 2000 Practical Recipes. (Beeton, 1923) [Hoyle 128]
Advice (p551-553; 565)
Beef tea, formerly regarded as the patient's greatest support, but now many doctors have ceased to attach much importance to it largely due to the difficulty of getting it properly prepared.

Eggs are a very valuable food … The white is equally nourishing and less rich than the yolk, and consequently may be given to the patient when the yolk would disagree.

Fish, being light and easily digested, plays an important part in invalid diet. Whiting, sole, flounder or plaice should be selected, as these contain a very small percentage of oily matter.

Meat juices and extracts may be bought ready prepared – some contain little more than the salines and extractives of the meat, others may be regarded as valuable stimulant and restorative.

Milk is undoubtedly a more valuable food for the sick than any kind of beef-tea, juice or essence.

Peptonised foods. Beef peptonoids and peptonised beef jelly are also most valuable preparations for the sick room. Unlike beef tea and beef extracts, which consist only of the juice of the meat more or less perfectly extracted, they are the meat itself in liquid form, fit to be taken at once into the body without any work for the feeble digestion.

The chief peptonizing agents are pepsin and liquor pancreaticus, and the food when acted upon becomes partially predigested and consequently more readily absorbed. When the natural digestive juices are deficient and the stomach is unable properly to perform its office, those who suffer from this cause may be employing one of these valuable agents, be supplied with more varied food than they would otherwise be able to digest.

Recipes (pp553-565)
- Beef essence
- Beef juice
- Beef tea and egg
- Beef tea custard
- Beef tea (2 recipes)
- Beef tea raw (this variety of beef tea is more easily digested than any other, in consequence of the albumen being contained in an uncooked and soluble condition)
- Calf's foot broth
- Chicken essence
- Eel broth
- Mutton broth
- Mutton tea
- Cod cutlets
- Fish cakes
- Fish fricassee
- Oysters, stewed
- Sole, grilled
- Whiting, boiled
- Whiting cream
- Whiting, steamed
- Calf's foot, stewed
- Chicken cream
- Chicken custard
- Chicken fillet, steamed
- Chicken or game, cooked, minced
- Chicken, raw minced
- Chicken panada
- Chop, steamed
- Egg, coddled
- Mutton, fresh minced
- Rabbit, stewed
- Raw beef balls
- Raw beef sandwiches
- Tripe, stewed
- Beef jelly
- Calf's foot jelly
- Egg jelly
- Irish moss jelly
- Milk jelly
- Restorative jelly
- Rice jelly
- Arrowroot soufflé
- Barley custard pudding
- Carrageen blancmange
- Custard mould

- Semolina cream
- Apple tea
- Arrowroot
- Barley gruel
- Barley water
- Blackcurrant tea
- Brandy and egg mixture
- Caudle
- Egg and brandy or wine
- Egg flip
- Eggnog
- Lemonade
- Lemon squash
- Lemon whey
- Linseed tea
- Oatmeal gruel
- Rice water
- Sago gruel
- Toast water
- Whey
- White of egg and soda water
- White wine whey
- Peptonised beef tea
- Peptonised beef tea jelly
- Peptonised gruel
- Peptonised milk
- Peptonised soups

1928. Mrs Beeton's Everyday Cookery with about 2500 Practical Recipes. (Beeton, 1928) [Hoyle 127]
Identical information and recipes

1950. Mrs. Beeton's Family Cookery with nearly 3000 Practical Recipes. (Beeton, 1950) [Not in Hoyle]
Identical information and recipes

1924

The Colonial Mutual Life Cookery Book.
(Colonial Mutual Life Assurance Society, 1924) [Hoyle 291]

Advice (p46)

The whole object of invalid cookery is to give the patient food suitable for the reduced strength, through illness, of the digestive system. It is impossible to lay down any rules of diet for sick people. The doctor alone can do this.

Recipes (pp46-47)
- Arrowroot
- Beef jelly
- Soups for invalids
- Beef tea
- Mutton broth
- Stewed tripe
- Boiled eggs

Davis Dainty Dishes (3rd edition). (Davis Gelatine (Australia), 1924) [Hoyle 355]
No invalid recipes

1937 Davis Dainty Dishes (Revised edition). (Davis Gelatine (Australia), 1937) [Hoyle 359]

Recipes (pp10-48)
- Jellied soup
- Angel's food [milk and egg]
- Egg jelly
- Golden parfait [eggs, honey, fruit juice]
- Honey jelly

98

- Lemon Bavarian
- Lemon jelly
- Lemon sponge
- Lemon whip
- Milk jelly
- Orange egg cream
- Prune gateau
- Rhubarb jelly
- Spanish cream
- Wine jelly

1940 (Reprinted edition) identical to 1937

1949 (Revised edition) No specific invalid recipes, but still included the same recipes under Children's section.

Everylady's Cook-Book (1ˢᵗ edition). (Drake, 1924) [Hoyle 418]
[Note: not the same as the *Everylady's Cook Book* (White, 1915)]

<u>Advice</u> (pp203-305)

[Extensive lesson on invalid cookery and the kinds of foods best suited to invalids, convalescents and children, including]:

Mutton is slightly less nourishing than beef but is more easily digested.

Salted meat, pork and veal are difficult to digest.

Bacon is a popular and wholesome form of fat. It should be toasted, grilled or well boiled, so do not use very lean bacon.

Poultry and game are tender, tempting, nourishing, and very easily digested. Do not give duck or goose unless specially ordered. They are too rich.

Fish is a valuable food. Choose the white-fleshed varieties, because more of the oil is stored in the liver of these fish, leaving an entire absence of fat in the flesh. Oily fish (though nourishing) often upsets the digestion.

Vegetables are necessary. Green ones especially; they contain Mineral Salts and more necessary still Vitamines. Without Vitamines no one can be perfectly healthy.

Milk contains Vitamines. Scalding it somewhat lessens its usefulness but is often necessary as a safeguard.

Oysters when eaten raw are nourishing and digestible. They can often be retained in the stomach, when other foods cause vomiting.

<u>Recipes</u> (pp205-214)
- Fried oysters
- Pigs in blankets
- Oysters
- Scalloped oysters
- Invalid grilled fish
- Beef tea (2 recipes)
- Raw beef tea
- Raw beef tea rolls
- Beef tea jelly
- Pulled bread
- "Egg bouillon"
- Mutton or chicken broth
- A very nourishing soup
- Chicken essence
- A delightful fish soup
- Sheep's trotters stewed
- Braised sweetbreads and bacon
- Stewed tripe
- Grilled steak
- Spatchcock
- To grill a joint of chicken
- Calves' or sheep's brains on toast
- Brains and bacon
- A steamed chop

- Boiled egg
- Buttered egg
- Egg jelly
- Steamed egg
- Scrambled egg
- Eggnog
- Junket
- Gruel
- Home made lemonade
- Cup custard
- Toast water
- Albumen water
- Barley water (2 recipes)
- Oyster sandwiches
- Raw beef sandwiches
- Marrow sandwiches or marrow on toast

193-? (2nd edition) identical recipes
1933? (4th edition) identical recipes
1934 (New and revised edition) identical recipes
1938 (Revised and popular edition) identical recipes

The Golden Wattle Cookery Book (1st edition). (Wylie, 1924) [Hoyle 1413]
<u>Advice</u> (p174)
General rules for invalid cookery
1. Food for the sick should be light, nourishing and easily digested.
2. Vary the food as much as possible. Use only the freshest ingredients.
3. Prepare only small quantities and so avoid waste.
4. Do not over sweeten or over flavour food.
5. Two Golden Rules are:
    - Give little food at a time and give it often
    - Serve it as daintily as possible
6. Never leave food in the sick room.
7. Do not present the same food a second time.
8. Remove every particle of fat from soups, broths or beef tea.
9. Serve meals punctually and carefully. Note the amount taken.
10. Avoid alcoholic drinks unless ordered by the doctor.
11. Perfect cleanliness is necessary in the preparation of food.

<u>Recipes</u> (pp174-183)
- Lemonade
- Arrowroot
- Orange jelly
- Siberian cream
- Apple jelly
- Fricassee of sweetbread
- Stewed brains
- Fried brains
- Fricassee of chicken
- Chicken cream
- Boiled chicken
- Milk jelly from cow heel
- Baked apples
- Stewed fruit
- White wine whey
- Toast water

1930 (3rd edition) (Wylie, 1930) [Hoyle 1414]
<u>Recipes</u> (pp200-212)
- Lemonade
- Milk arrowroot
- Water arrowroot
- Egg flip

- Barley water (2 recipes)
- Gruel
- Raw beef tea
- Beef essence
- Beef tea (2 recipes)
- Mutton broth
- Chicken broth
- Celery soup
- Lemon sponge
- Orange jelly
- Siberian cream
- Apple jelly
- Fricassee of sweetbread
- Stewed brains
- Fried brains
- Fricassee of chicken
- Chicken cream
- Boiled chicken
- Milk jelly from cow heel
- Steamed egg
- Baked apples
- Stewed fruit
- White wine whey
- Toast water

1931 (4th edition) (Wylie, 1931) [Hoyle 1415] identical recipes <u>plus</u> Steamed custard
1940 (7th edition) identical recipes <u>plus</u> Steamed fish
1969 (20th edition) identical to 7th edition
2005 (36th edition) identical to 20th edition but missing: Toast water and Steamed custard

The Housewife's Shopping Guide and Cookery Book.
(The Progressive Publicity Company, 1924) [Hoyle 672]
<u>Recipes</u> (pp77-83 and 117-118)

- Invalid's soup
- Chicken broth for invalids
- Arrowroot made with milk
- Beef essence
- Beef tea
- To stew a chop
- Raw beef tea
- White broth
- To grill a chop
- Beef tea custard

Kindergarten Cookery Book (2nd edition).
(Kindergarten Union of New South Wales, 1924) [Hoyle 710]
<u>Recipes</u> (pp145-154)

- Apple water
- Barley water
- Beef tea
- Blackcurrant tea
- Celery soup
- Egg flip (2 recipes)
- Gruel
- Mutton broth
- White of egg
- Baked eggs
- Baked egg and tomatoes
- Steamed eggs
- Beef tea or savoury custard
- Baked fish
- Fried fish
- Scalloped fish
- Steamed whiting
- Fried brains
- Scalloped brains
- Stewed chicken
- Baked loin chops
- Baked potatoes
- Stuffed tomato
- White sauce
- Baked apples
- Batter pudding

- Baked custard
- Boiled custard
- Steamed custard
- Cup of arrowroot or cornflour
- Cup of sago
- Tapioca custard
- Stewed fruit
- Junket
- Gluten bread
- Fruit jelly
- Lemon meringue
- Steamed sponge pudding
- Cream sandwich
- Sultana or plain cake

Miss Futter's Australian Home Cookery (2nd edition). (Futter, 1924) [Hoyle 556]
[No separate section, but the following recipes are included in the Miscellaneous Hints]
<u>Recipes</u> (pp186-187)
- Apple water
- Barley water for invalids
- Rice water
- Gruel (2 recipes)
- Whipped junket for invalids
- Meat collops (for invalids)
- Gravy beef (for invalids)
- How to make raw meat juice
- Albumen water

1926 (3rd edition) identical to 2nd edition with one addition
- A good invalid's food [flour and junket tablets]

1934 (4th edition) identical to 3rd edition

Recipes: Secret, selected, practical, original. (The Wardmaster, 1924) [Hoyle 1340]
<u>Advice</u> (no page numbers)
Sick persons should never be asked what they will have to eat, but bring them something suitable and unexpected.

Never leave food lying about a sick room. Serve as "daintily" as possible.

<u>Recipes</u> (no page numbers)
- Omelette
- Chicken broth
- Mutton broth
- Raw beef tea
- Steamed chop
- Steamed fish
- Arrowroot jelly
- Egg flip
- Albumen water ("This is useful in cases of vomiting")
- Invalid pudding

Simple Cookery for Use in Itinerant Domestic Schools. (Queensland Department of Public Instruction, 1924) [Hoyle 1111]
<u>Recipes</u> [No separate section but includes the following recipes]:
- Beef tea (Lesson VI.b)
- Arrowroot (Lesson XIV.e)
- Barley water (Lesson XIV.g)
- Toast water (Lesson XIV.h)

South Australian Presbyterian Cookery Book.
(Chalmers Church Friendship Club, 1924) [Hoyle 1090]
Advice (p59)
Don't walk in a sick room, glide and wear rubbers on heels; close doors quietly and speak quietly. Do not leave food in a patient's room or on kitchen table for flies to crawl over; put food away or use a net or butter cloth over same.

Recipes (pp59-60)
- Salsify and oyster plant soup
- Artichoke soup
- Large bean soup
- Lentil
- Boiled onions

To Mr. and Mrs. Newlywed. (Anon, 1924) [Hoyle 1300]
Advice (p141)
In preparing her diet the greatest care should be taken, never giving too much or too often the same kind of food. Prepare it daintily and serve it daintily, and if not consumed take it out of the sick-room at once.

Avoid all kinds of fats and greases and, if milk is ordered, be sure you have it fresh on hand for whenever it is required.

It is really difficult to give an invalid constant changes, but a little thought and care will always find you some fresh dish that is suitable.

Recipes (p131)
- Raw beef tea
- Beef tea
- Mutton broth
- Chicken broth
- Toast water
- Thick barley water
- Rice water
- Stewed oysters

1925

"All in One" Recipe Book and Household Guide. (Cox, 1925) [Hoyle 373]
Recipes (Numbers 271-291)
- Albumen water
- Arrowroot jelly
- Apple delight
- Apple water
- Baked apple
- Beef tea custard
- Chicken broth
- Clear barley water
- Egg flip
- Gruel
- Invalid pudding
- Lemon drink
- Light bread pudding
- Mutton broth
- Omelette
- Raw beef tea
- Steamed chop
- Steamed custard
- Steamed fish
- Toast water

The Barker College Cookery Book. (Turner, 1925) [Hoyle 104]
<u>Recipes</u> (pp73-74)
- Beef tea
- Chicken broth
- Fried sweetbreads
- Fried brains
- Ground rice
- Mutton broth
- Port wine jelly
- Steamed sweetbreads
- Tripe in milk

Green and Gold Cookery Book (2nd edition). (Anon, 1925) [Hoyle 592]
<u>Recipes</u> (pp197-199)
- Barley water
- Cup of cornflour or arrowroot
- Cup of gruel
- Beef tea (2 recipes)
- Raw beef tea
- Beef tea custard
- Boiled sago
- Chicken broth
- Drink for invalids
- Egg flip
- Fricasseed brains
- Lemonade
- Light bread pudding
- Mutton broth
- Steamed custard
- Steamed fish
- Treacle posset (for a cold)

1927 (**3rd edition**) identical recipes
1928 (**4th edition**) identical recipes
1932 (**6th edition**) identical recipes
1938 (**9th edition**) identical recipes
1938 (**10th edition**) identical recipes
1939 (**11th edition**) identical recipes <u>plus</u> milk jelly
1940 (**12th edition**) identical to the 11th edition
1942 (**14th edition**) identical to the 11th edition
1944 (**18th edition**) identical to the 11th edition
1948 (**21st edition**) identical to the 11th edition
1949 (**22nd edition**) identical to the 11th edition
1951? (**24th edition**) identical to the 11th edition
1954 (**26th edition**) identical to the 11th edition
196-? (**28th edition**) identical to the 11th edition
1967 (**31st edition**) identical to the 11th edition
197-? (**39th edition**) identical to the 11th edition
1983 (**40th edition**) identical to the 11th edition
1985 (**41st edition**) identical to the 11th edition
1999 (**75th Anniversary edition**) identical to the 11th edition

Home Nursing: Feeding the convalescent. (Dateba, 1925) [Not in Hoyle]
<u>Advice</u> (p21)
More difficult than feeding the really sick person is feeding of the convalescent. It is often hard to please them in this weakened state. A little food often is a good rule to follow.

Florence Nightingale said that one of the most common errors among the women in charge of sick persons was their belief that beef-tea was nourishing. There is very little nourishment in beef-tea. It is usually classed among the mild stimulants. Calves-foot jelly is another article whose nourishing properties are over-estimated. By making gelatine into a certain bulk by adding water to it you don't add that amount of nourishment.

It is an odd saying that "an egg is worth a pound of meat". It isn't. It is doubtful whether, weight for weight, eggs are equal to beef-steak.

Recipes (p21)
- Beef tea and extracts
- Beef juice
- Milk albumen
- Barley water
- Mulled wine

Miss Drake's Home Cookery (6th edition). (Drake, 1925) [Hoyle 428]
Recipes (pp124-127)
- Barley water (2 recipes)
- Beef tea (2 recipes)
- Beef tea raw
- Chicken broth
- Cup custard
- Gruel
- Home made lemonade
- Grilled fish
- Mutton broth
- Steamed egg
- Toast water
- Various meals for an invalid from one chicken or fowl

1929? (7th edition) Invalid cookery section not included. Readers are referred to her book "Dainty Dishes"
1943 (11th edition) identical to 7th edition
1950 (13th edition) identical to 7th edition

Strathalbyn Cookery Book No 2. (Edgar, 1925) [Hoyle 470]
Recipes (pp 40-41)
- Barley water
- Rice water
- Oatmeal water
- Beef broth
- Rice milk
- Lemon milk sherbet
- Oyster stew
- Whey
- Jellied chicken

1926

"Carry On" Cookery Book (5th edition). (King, 1926) [Hoyle 715]
Advice (pp140-146) Medical Hints including:
- Onion gruel for colds
- Linseed tea (invaluable for colds and sore throats)
- Beef extract in wine (very beneficial in cases of great weakness or exhaustion)

1949 (9th edition). No invalid diet information

Cookery Book. (Fletcher Chester & Co, 1926) [Hoyle 507]
Recipes (pp89-95)
- Gruel
- Beef tea (2 recipes)
- Beef jelly
- Mutton broth
- Beef tea with egg
- Apple water
- Egg drink
- Spatchcock
- Omelette
- Light pudding
- Rice water
- Linseed tea
- A gargle for the throat

1928 No invalid recipes

Cooking Craft. (Nash, 1926) [Hoyle 931]
Advice (pp250-251)

Choose foods suitable to the illness or ailment which will supply the necessary nutriment to replace normal or excessive wastage; this should be in small bulk, as an invalid's appetite is usually slender.

Select those articles of food which are most easily digested, and prepare them in the most digestible manner, so there is no risk of unduly taxing the often already weakened digestive system, which in an illness is more or less impaired.

Seasoning and flavouring must be delicate. Pepper should not generally be used; vegetables, which tend to create flatulency, should be used judiciously and sparingly, either of flavouring or for service separately. Over-sweetening is likewise to be avoided. Food should never be accompanied by rich, highly-seasoned sauces.

Prepare foods preferably by steaming or stewing; frying is to be avoided except when convalescence is advanced.

In all cases of severe illness always have some nourishment or a beverage in readiness such as broth, beef tea, jelly, barley water, lemonade etc.

Recipes (pp252-257)
- Beef tea (2 recipes)
- Raw beef tea
- Beef tea jelly
- Gruel
- Cup of arrowroot
- Barley water (2 recipes)
- White wine whey
- Lemon whey
- Buttermilk whey
- Peptonised milk
- Peptonised gruel

1937 (3rd edition) identical contents to 1926

Mrs Carter's Cookery Book. (Carter, 1926) [Hoyle 214]
Recipes (pp37-38)
- Invalid wafer biscuits
- Veal jelly
- Boiled milk for invalids
- Broiled chicken for invalids
- Invalid tart
- Tripe fricassee

Principles of Home Cookery. (The New South Wales Public School Cookery Teachers' Association, 1926) [Not in Hoyle]

Advice (pp47-48)

[General comments (not recipes) including]:

A convalescent is a person who is recovering from an illness.

Very careful dieting is necessary to rebuild the body, which has been weakened by the illness. The digestion is still weak, so care must be taken not to overtax it. The return to ordinary diet must be gradual.

The lightest methods of cooking should be used, namely steaming, grilling and boiling, and variety be introduced in the methods of cooking and serving.

Included in the dishes usually served are light soups and broths, oysters, brains, chicken, tripe, milk puddings, custards, junket, jelly, baked apples, prunes etc. Avoid too much starchy food.

1927 (2nd edition) identical information
1931 (7th edition) identical information
1933 (10th edition) identical information
1939 (11th edition) identical information
1941 (19th edition) identical information

1927

The Best of Everything Recipe Book. (The Disabled Mens' Association, 1927) [Hoyle 376]

Recipes (Numbers 155-181)

- Albumen water
- Arrowroot jelly
- Apple delight
- Apple water
- Baked apple
- Beef tea custard
- Good beef tea
- Chicken broth
- Clear barley water
- Egg flip
- Eggnog or beaten egg
- Invalid pudding
- Lemon drink
- Light bread pudding
- Mutton broth
- Omelette
- Raw beef tea
- Steamed chop
- Steamed custard
- Steamed fish
- Lamb's sweetbreads
- Creamed sweetbreads
- Frothed egg
- Rice water
- Lemonade
- Whey
- Wine whey

Canberra Cookery Book of Good and Tried Recipes. (Anon, 1927) [Hoyle 211]

Recipes (pp178-184)

- Beef tea (2 recipes)
- Mutton broth
- Veal broth
- Chicken broth
- Fish in milk
- Steamed fish
- Meat jelly
- Steamed chop

- Beef quenelles
- Steamed custard
- Savoury custard
- Port wine jelly
- Orange jelly
- Milk jelly
- Junket
- Arrowroot pudding
- Cup of cornflour
- Lemonade
- Barley water
- Blackcurrant tea
- Linseed tea
- Gruel
- Treacle posset
- Toast water
- Egg and milk

Electric Refrigerator Recipes and Menus. (Bradley & others, 1927) [Hoyle 68]
Recipes (p59)
- Frapped grape juice
- Frapped sherry milk
- Orange ice for diabetics
- Frapped chicken broth
- Other diabetic dishes
  - Tomato frappe
  - Strawberry milk sherbet
- Lemon cream sherbet
- Vanilla mousse
- Peach mousse
- Orange pekoe mousse
- Milk mousse
- Coffee ice cream with evaporated milk

The Mary Elizabeth Cook Book. (Aronson, 1927) [Hoyle 51]
Recipes (pp185-188)
- Chicken broth with chicken and rice
- Tripe for an invalid
- Broiled whiting
- Beef essence
- Savoury gruel
- White wine whey
- Boiled sole
- An excellent pick-me-up
- Beef jelly
- Barley water
- Prune water
- Savoury custard
- Rice and milk
- Chicken broth
- Chicken jelly
- Invalid chop
- Port wine jelly
- Beef tea for convalescents
- Invalid's boiled custard
- Apple tea
- Groat's gruel

1928

Manual of Domestic Art (Cookery). (Education Department of South Australia, 1928) [Hoyle 1257]
Advice (p105)
[Rules for diets including 5 classes of diets: Ordinary Full, Low, Milk, Light and Meat.]

Recipes (pp106-110)
- Steamed fish
- Sago cream
- Gruel
- Steamed custard
- Lemonade
- Barley water
- Beef tea (2 recipes)
- Egg flip
- Steamed egg
- Fricasseed brains
- Junket
- Milk jelly (2 recipes)
- Toast water
- Clear barley water
- Invalid broth
- Sago cream soup
- Apple water
- Beef tea custard
- Light bread pudding
- Restorative jelly

1929 identical to 1928 edition
1932 identical to 1928 edition
1937 identical to 1928 edition
1946 identical to 1928 edition
1951 identical to 1928 edition

The Mission Cookery Book. (The Mission of St James and St John, 1928) [Hoyle 873]
Recipes (pp169-175)
- Arrowroot
- Beef tea
- Barley water
- Bread pudding
- Brain cutlets
- Calf's foot jelly
- Cup pudding
- To grill or joint a chicken
- Chicken cream
- Cheese omelette
- Eggs and tomatoes
- Gruel
- Junket
- Linseed tea
- Lemon jelly
- Mutton jelly
- Mutton broth
- Nut fritters
- Oatmeal or wheatmeal jelly
- Rice water
- Steamed rice
- Strengthening broth
- Stewed chop
- Sweetbreads
- Tripe and milk
- Tripe

The Star Cookery Book. (The Disabled Mens' Association, 1928) [Hoyle 395]
Recipes (Numbers 1-7)
- Albumen water
- Arrowroot jelly
- Egg flip
- Invalid pudding
- Raw beef tea
- Steamed chop
- Steamed fish

1929

Invalid Cookery. (Queensland Department of Public Instruction, 1929) [Not in Hoyle]

Advice (pp1-9)

General advice on feeding invalids – mainly for nurses – and specific information on foods allowed and not allowed for various diseases (Appendicitis, Bright's disease, bronchitis, constipation, consumption, diabetes, diarrhoea, dyspepsia, eczema, typhoid fever, gastritis, gout, heart disease, obesity, pneumonia, rheumatism).

Recipes (pp9-52)

- Albumen water
- Apple water
- Barley water
- Blackcurrant tea
- Chocolate
- Lemonade
- Lemon whey
- Oatmeal drink
- Rice water
- Toast water
- Peptonised beef tea/gruel/milk
- Beef, chicken and veal essences
- Beef tea custard
- Beef tea and white of egg
- Beef tea (3 recipes)
- Raw beef tea
- Beef sandwich (raw)
- Beef cakes
- Mutton broth
- Chicken or veal broth
- Rice soup
- Vermicelli soup
- Fish soup
- Tomato soup
- Oyster soup
- Boiled green peas
- Asparagus or celery
- Boiled onions with white sauce
- Lima beans, haricot beans or lentils
- Steamed vegetables – pumpkin potatoes and marrow
- Boiled French beans
- Boiled cabbage
- Potatoes mashed or flaked
- Boiled marrow or pumpkin
- Tomato pie
- Sweet sauce
- Tomato sauce
- Gravy
- Mayonnaise
- Caramel sauce
- White sauce
- Cheese sauce
- Egg sauce
- Parsley sauce
- Lemon sauce
- Bread sauce
- Dutch sauce
- Brown sauce
- Fish fried in four ways
- Fish poached in milk
- Steamed fish
- Baked fish
- Grilled fish
- Quenelles of fish
- Fish creams
- Fish pie
- Kedgeree
- Fish and tomatoes
- Rolled whiting
- Fish cakes
- Fish au gratin
- Salmon pie
- Oysters devilled
- Oysters in tomato
- Oysters and potato
- Oyster pie
- Scalloped oysters

- Oysters in shells
- Oysters au gratin
- Steamed oysters
- Stewed tripe
- Steamed boned chop
- Braised sweetbread
- Stewed brains
- Fried brains
- Invalid mince
- Lamb cutlet
- Veal creams
- Quenelles of beef
- Grilled fillet
- Grilled chop
- Baked chop in paper case
- Grilled invalid mince
- Toasted bacon
- Boiled egg
- Egg flip
- Soufflé
- Omelette
- Prairie egg
- Bake egg in tomato
- Scrambled egg
- Steamed egg
- Poached egg
- Steamed batter pudding
- Canadian eggs
- Savoury egg and tomato
- Fricassee of chicken
- Chicken creams
- Quenelles of chicken
- Steamed chicken
- Baked chicken
- Chicken rissoles or cutlets
- Steamed chicken and tomato sauce
- Wine or lemon jelly
- Lemon sponge
- Farinaceous jelly
- Calf's foot jelly
- Sponge cake
- Rusks
- Milk jelly
- Arrowroot
- Madeira cake
- Gruel (2 recipes)
- Oatmeal jelly
- Bread and milk
- Bread jelly
- Toast
- Buttered toast
- Baked rice
- Boiled custard
- Sago custard
- Bread and butter custard
- Steamed pudding
- Benger's food
- Junket
- Baked apple
- Steamed apples
- Baked custard
- Rice custard

1930-1939

School of Mines Cookery Book (Ross, Batchelor, Kinnear, & Crossley, 1936)

The New PWMU Cookery Book (Campbell, 1936)

193-?

Australian Home Cookery. (Prudence, 193-?) [Hoyle 1109]

<u>Advice</u> (p342)

Meals for the invalid or convalescent should be as attractive as possible.

Serve small helpings and serve in such a way that they may be partaken of easily and without undue bother.

Individual dishes look, and are, much better than a helping from a large dish. The food should be varied as often as possible, as everything so soon becomes monotonous for an invalid. Because the patient likes a certain dish, do not serve it continually.

Never ask the patient what he or she likes or dislikes; let each dish be in the nature of a surprise.

If onions are included in a dish they should be blanched. Fish should be filleted. Fried food should not be given. Oysters are more digestible and nutritious when raw.

Savoury custards make a change. Omit the sugar, season with pepper and salt, and add finely grated cheese or a little meat extract. Jelly and blanc-mange take on a different air when whipped. Mashed potato may be made to look different and attractive. Fork it into pyramids, and bake on a buttered slide, in a hot oven, till lightly browned.

<u>Recipes</u> (pp342-437)
- Mutton broth
- Invalid's broth
- Beef tea
- Raw beef tea
- Barley water (2 recipes)
- Orange drink
- Egg flip
- Fish eggs
- Mock whitebait
- Baked bream
- Beef mince
- Coddled egg
- Steamed egg
- Tripe custard
- Snow custard
- Peach foam
- Apple soufflé
- Apple blancmange

Electric Cookery Book. (State Electricity Commission of Victoria, 193-?) [Hoyle 1266]

<u>Recipes</u> (p69)
- Barley water
- Oatmeal gruel
- Junket
- Beef tea
- Egg flip

The Home Golden Cookery Book. (Anon, 193-?-a) [Hoyle 577]

<u>Recipes</u> (p109-117)
- Beef tea
- Meat juice
- Egg flip
- Egg jelly
- Meat jelly
- Oatmeal jelly
- Oatmeal gruel
- Invalid's pudding
- Fish for an invalid
- Poached egg in milk

- To boil an egg
- Toast
- Arrowroot, made with milk
- Arrowroot, made with water
- Milk toast
- Broth for an invalid
- Mutton broth
- Invalid custard
- Custard savoury
- Tripe
- Sheep's brains
- Grilled chicken
- Chicken broth
- Steamed fish
- Chop
- Oatmeal water
- Linseed tea
- Rice water
- Beef tea and oatmeal
- Lemonade
- Bran tea
- Barley water (2 recipes)
- Egg lemonade
- Egg drink
- Soda, milk, and egg
- Apple water (2 recipes)
- Rhubarb water
- Blackcurrant drink
- Hot lemonade
- Pineapple lemonade
- Prune water
- Toast water

Marmite Recipes: Marmite cookery book. (Sanitarium Health Food Company, 193-?) [Hoyle 1204]

<u>Advice</u> (p11)
General Directions for Use of Marmite
1. Seasoning is better withheld in many forms of illness, such as throat and chest infections. Many patients crave something tasty. Marmite supplies this want and comes as a boon to those who have been fed or nourished for any length of time on an insipid diet, both liquid and solid.
2. Marmite is an excellent standby in convalescence because all sorts of foods, e.g. eggs, cereals, and vegetables, either singly or in combination may be enriched in dietetic value, and changed in flavour and appearance by its aid. The good results obtained by a little ingenuity are known to all who have had any experience in sick nursing.
3. Marmite may be blended with cream or milk, either to be taken hot or cold, or tepid. In the latter form, milk alone if often distasteful; with Marmite it agrees better as a rule.

<u>Recipes</u> (pp12-14)
- Nourishing savoury custard
- Nourishing jelly
- Invalid soup
- Savoury soufflé
- Marmite toast
- Marmite arrowroot
- Albumen water
- Mulled milk
- Marmite butter
- Vegetarian soup
- Bayo bean and celery

Recipe Book: Containing all the best culinary recipes, formulas and menus. (The Disabled Mens' Association, 193-?) [Hoyle 394]

Recipes (pp44-46)

- Albumen water
- Arrowroot jelly
- Apple delight
- Apple water
- Baked apple
- Beef tea custard
- Chicken broth
- Clear barley water
- Baked bream
- Beef mince
- Coddled egg
- Steamed egg
- Tripe custard
- Egg flip
- Gruel
- Invalid pudding
- Lemon drink
- Light bread pudding
- Mutton broth
- Omelette
- Raw beef tea
- Snow custard
- Peach foam
- Apple soufflé
- Apple blancmange

Whitcombe's Everyday Cookery: 1062 selected and tested recipes, revised by cookery experts and leading dietitians. (Anon, 193-?-b)[Hoyle 1352]

Advice (p300)
[General advice on Food for the Sick]

Recipes (pp300-302)

- Lemonade
- Orangeade
- Sherry and egg
- Eggnog
- Ginger milk
- Cocoa
- Barley water
- Porridge
- Arrowroot
- Chicken broth
- Beef tea
- Poultry, rabbits, brains, sweetbreads – steam or serve as fricassee with white sauce
- Steamed or grilled fish
- Lamb chops, loin chops – grill or bake (without fat)
- Eggs – coddle, poach or scramble
- Cream vegetable soups
- Fruit soufflés
- Fruit whip
- Jellies
- Ice cream
- Sponge cake (plain)
- Stewed fruit
- Baked fruit

1945 (Wartime edition) [Hoyle 1352]
Identical contents about Food for the Sick as the 193-? edition.

Between 1930 and 1935

Invalid and Convalescent Cookery for Hospital Trainees (2nd edition).
(Butler, Between 1930 and 1935) [Hoyle 205]

[A textbook containing lecture notes and recipes for hospital trainees taking the Australasian Trained Nurse Association examination, in which a course of Invalid Cookery was compulsory]

Advice (p5)
1. Food for invalids and convalescents must be nourishing and easily digested; it must be readily assimilated in the body without unduly taxing the digestive organs which have been weakened by illness.
2. The food should be varied as much as possible within the prescribed diet. Endeavour to avoid monotony.
3. The necessary amount of food, the quality of the ingredients, the correct food values, skillful cooking, and daintiness in serving, are important factors to be considered in an invalid's diet.
4. Aim at making the invalid's tray attractive to the eye (well polished silver, glass, and china; well laundered linen; food daintily served). Food pleasing in appearance tempts the appetite.
5. Do not consult the patient about food. Prepare (within the prescribed diet) what you think will be liked, and let it come as a surprise.
6. Serve in small quantities. Do not present the same food twice in succession. Serve hot foods really hot, and cold foods cold. Use seasonings sparingly.
7. Always have something in readiness, such as soup, jelly, or a refreshing drink.
8. Remove all dishes and untouched food from the sick-room as soon as the patient's appetite is appeased.
9. Freshness of ingredients and perfect cleanliness in their preparation are absolutely necessary.
10. It is advisable to have a little nourishment or stimulant to be given immediately after the fatigue of sponging or dressing, such as a cup of hot milk, or beef tea with the addition of one or two teaspoons of brandy.
11. To the convalescent, food should be something more than physical nourishment; something beyond a mere collection of carbohydrates, proteins and fats. It should transcend calories, vitamins and roughages, and become to the body as a poem to the ear, satisfying, stimulating – a fillip to the imagination. Plain wholesome food may be *sustenance*, but in dealing with tissues that are brought back to a normal state, there should be an admixture of the vitamins of *art*. Food should appeal to the senses jaded by disease, and be as nourishment to the spirit as to the body.

Common fallacies concerning food (p10-11)
- **Broth** unfortunately and incorrectly conveys to most minds that idea of a food of high nutritive value. Clear meat broth averages 90% water! Broth is a mild stimulant to the gastric digestion, and therefore should be included in moderation in an invalid's diet. It leaves a feeling of fullness and satisfaction, without appreciable nourishment.
- **Beef tea** is a stimulant, not a food. It whips up flagging vitality by stimulating the nervous and bodily activities, but it does not *supply* vitality; it merely calls latent vitality into action by stimulating the nervous system. It must not be relied on for nourishment.

- **Raw egg white**. We have long considered raw eggs a highly valuable food. As far as raw white of egg is concerned, recent experience tends to prove that it is not always advisable to give patients raw egg white. It is true that raw egg-white leaves the stomach rapidly, though not because it is quickly digested (as was once considered) but because it actually resists digestive action … This fact should cause us to discontinue the practice of giving raw egg white to diarrhoeal conditions, and to make less frequent use of albuminoid drinks. Raw egg-yolk and cooked eggs show no such tendency. Egg flips are therefore better made with yolks only, or, if using whites also, yolks and whites should be beaten separately, the milk quite hot and poured onto the beaten egg white (thus partly cooking it and rendering it more digestible, and the beaten yolk added last.

<u>Recipes</u> (pp21-96)

Cooling drinks
- Albumen water
- Albumenised milk
- Apple water
- Barley water (2 recipes)
- Lemonade
- Lemon squash
- Orangeade
- Prune drink
- Rice water
- Toast water

Nourishing and stimulating drinks
- Arrowroot
- Barley gruel
- Beef tea gruel
- Egg flip (2 recipes)
- Egg flip (yolk only)
- Egg brandy
- Gruel (2 recipes)
- Milk and suet
- Whey
- Wine whey

Beef tea, broths and soups
- Barley cream soup
- Beef tea (2 recipes)
- Beef tea with milk
- Beef tea custard
- Beef tea jelly
- Celery cream soup
- Celery and barley soup
- Chicken broth
- Mutton broth
- Raw beef tea
- Veal broth

Fish
- Boiled fish
- Fillets of whiting on toast
- Fricassee of oysters
- Fried fish
- Grilled whiting
- Oysters on toast
- Scalloped oysters
- Steamed fish
- Stewed whiting
- White sauce

Milk, eggs, fats, sugar, starchy foods
- Apple Charlotte
- Baked rice pudding
- Baked macaroni or vermicelli custard
- Baked custard
- Baked bread and butter custard
- Baked rice custard
- Baked sago custard
- Boiled custard
- Boiled cornflour custard
- Sago cream
- Semolina cream
- Steamed custard

Stewed meats, liver cookery
- Fricassee of sweetbread
- Fricassee of brains
- Fried brains
- Fried sweetbreads
- Liver cocktail
- Liver extract
- Liver on toast
- Raw liver juice
- Raw liver sandwiches
- Savoury minced liver on toast
- Steamed liver mould
- Stewed tripe
- Stewed rabbit
- Stewed chops

Grilled and baked meats, liver cookery, vegetables
- Baked chicken
- Boiled chicken
- Boiled celery
- Broiled (grilled) liver
- Calf's liver hashed
- Fricassee of chicken
- French beans
- Fried liver and bacon
- Grilled chicken
- Green peas
- Green peas with carrots
- Liver paste
- Liver and ham en casserole
- Mashed carrots or parsnips
- Mashed potatoes
- Spinach puree
- White onions

Fruit, peptonising
- Baked apples
- Junket
- Omelettes
- Peptonised milk
- Poached egg
- Savoury omelette (2 recipes)
- Stewed apples
- Stewed rhubarb
- Stewed peaches
- Sweet omelette

Cold sweets, jellies and creams
- Caramel cream
- Egg jelly (blancmange)
- Lemon pudding
- Lemon sponge
- Milk jelly
- Siberian cream (or Angel's food)
- Spanish cream

Puddings
- Albert pudding
- Apple snow
- Lemon sago snow
- Lemon snow
- Milk sago snow
- Queen pudding
- Steamed caramel custard
- Steamed cabinet pudding
- Sweet white sauce

Supplementary recipes
- Apricot gateau
- Arrowroot sauce
- Arrowroot pudding
- Bacon rolls on buttered toast
- Baked liver and bacon
- Baked liver with vegetables
- Baked calf's liver, stuffed
- Beef tea pudding
- Brain cakes
- Bread and milk
- Braised liver
- Butter sauce
- Bubble bread
- Butterfly cakes

- Cheese and egg toast
- Chicken custard
- Chicken cream
- Chicken or rabbit liver soufflés
- Coffee rolls
- Cornflour cakes
- Egg in tomato
- Egg in bread sauce
- Egg in gravy
- Fished stewed in milk
- Fish soup
- Fricassee of oysters
- Fried liver with onions
- Frothed egg
- Gem scones
- Grilled pigeon
- Jellied rabbit
- Koumiss
- Kidney mince
- Lamb's liver (whole) en casserole
- Lemon whey
- Liver paste
- Liver en casserole
- Liver a la McAlpin
- Liver a la Francaise
- Liver and vegetables en casserole
- Little fruit cakes
- Macaroni and tomatoes
- Marrow rings
- Milk tea (2 recipes)
- Milk soup
- Orange sauce
- Oyster soup
- Poached egg with mince
- Poached egg with tomato
- Prairie oysters
- Raw beef sandwiches
- Savoury liver
- Savoury liver, baked
- Sago cream soup
- Scalloped oysters
- Scones
- Scrambled eggs
- Steamed fish pudding
- Stewed pigeon
- Tasty sandwiches
- Treacle posset
- Veal or rabbit cream

Marmite. (Sanitarium Health Food Company, Between 1930 and 1935) [Hoyle 1203]
<u>Advice</u> (p11).
[General directions on the use of Marmite for invalids]

<u>Recipes</u> (pp12-14)
- Nourishing custard
- Nourishing jelly
- Invalid soup
- Marmite toasts
- Marmite arrowroot

1930?

Milk Recipes. (Milk Board Sydney, 1930?) [Hoyle 860]
<u>Recipes</u> (pp34-35)
- Angel's food
- Arrowroot
- Creamed fish
- Gruel
- Junkets
- Light bread pudding
- Savoury liver custard
- Milk jelly

121

1930

Citrus Recipes for Every Day. (The Victorian Railways Commissioners in conjuction with The Victorian Central Citrus Association, 1930) [Hoyle 231]

Advice (p62).

When cooking for the sick and convalescent, the appearance and flavour of foods must be given particular care. It is usually necessary to appeal to a wavering appetite and to provide a tempting variety while still remaining within the limits of the physician's orders.

Oranges and lemons are acceptable to almost every palate. Their delicious, slightly acid flavour awakens and stimulates the appetite, and their natural salts and acids aid digestion.

Although known as 'acid foods' their reaction in the body is alkaline, so that they serve to balance eggs, fish, meat and other protein foods, and thus act as an aid to proper nutrition, which is important in the building up of the convalescent's strength.

Recipes (pp62-63)

- Lemonade
- Orangeade
- Grapefruit and orange salad
- Lemon gelatine
- Orange gelatine
- Orange tapioca pudding
- Orange ice
- Orange ice cream
- Orange omelette
- Hot lemonade
- Lemon whey
- Baked orange for a cold

1933 edition identical recipes

1948 edition. (The Victorian Railways Commissioner for the Federal Citrus Council of Australia, 1948) [Hoyle 235]

Identical but without lemonade and orangeade <u>plus</u> lemon cup, orange cup, orange eggnog, and egg lemon squash.

School of Mines Cookery Book (1st edition). (Ross, Batchelor, Kinnear, & Crossley, 1930) [Hoyle 1157]

Advice (pp215-218)

[General advice on invalid cookery and nutrition information]

Recipes (pp218-225)

- Lemonade
- Orangeade
- Apple water
- Barley water (2 recipes)
- Egg flip
- White wine whey
- Treacle posset
- Albuminised milk or water
- Gruel
- Milk puddings
- Sago or tapioca custard
- Sago or tapioca cream
- Steamed custard
- Baked custard
- Custard
- Mutton broth
- Chicken broth
- Beef tea (2 recipes)
- Raw beef tea
- Beef essence
- Sago cream soup
- Steamed fish

- White sauce for fish
- Fish baked in milk
- Mashed potatoes
- Savoury omelette
- Sweet omelette
- Poached egg on toast
- Junket
- Canary pudding
- Sweet sauce
- Caramel custard
- Queen pudding
- Cup of arrowroot or cornflour
- Baked apple
- Stewed fruits
- Tripe and onions
- Fried brains
- Fricassee brains
- Sweetbreads
- Lemon jelly
- Siberian cream
- Blancmange
- Orange jelly
- Boiled fowl
- Parsley sauce
- Baked fowl
- Bread sauce
- Brown gravy

1936 (2nd edition) (Ross et al., 1936) [Hoyle 1158]

<u>Advice</u> (pp247-251)

[Information about general rules of invalid cookery and food values]

<u>Recipes</u> (pp251-273)

- Lemonade
- Apple water
- Barley water (thick)
- Egg drink
- White wine whey
- Albuminised milk or water
- Gruel
- Linseed tea
- Milk puddings
- Rice and macaroni custard
- Sago or tapioca custard
- Sago or tapioca cream
- Custard
- Baked custard
- Invalid fruit tart
- Queen pudding
- Creamed rice
- Bread and butter pudding
- Vanilla soufflé
- Mutton broth
- Chicken broth
- Beef tea (3 recipes)
- Raw beef tea
- Beef tea custard
- Beef essence
- Sago soup
- Liver broiled
- Liver and tomatoes
- Raw liver pulp
- Liver balls
- Raw liver sandwiches
- Liver minced
- Liver soufflé
- Steamed fish
- White sauce for fish
- Fish baked in milk
- Fried fish
- Scalloped fish
- Oysters
- Fricassee of oysters
- Omelettes
- Savoury omelette
- Sweet omelette
- Poached egg on toast
- Sultana pudding
- Sweet sauce
- Caramel custard
- Cup of arrowroot or cornflour

- Junket
- Baked apple
- Stewed fruits
- Tripe and onions
- Fried brains
- Fricassee brains
- Fricassee of sweetbreads
- Lemon jelly
- Orange jelly
- Port wine jelly
- Prune jelly
- Russian jelly
- Calf's foot jelly
- Siberian cream
- Fig custard
- Blancmange
- Boiled fowl
- Parsley sauce
- Baked fowl
- Bread sauce
- Brown sauce

1944 (3rd edition) (Ross, Batchelor, Kinnear, & Crossley, 1944) [Not in Hoyle]

<u>Recipes</u> (pp226-245)

- Lemonade
- Barley water
- Egg drink
- Gruel
- Mutton broth
- Chicken broth
- Beef tea (3 recipes)
- Raw beef tea
- Beef tea custard
- Beef essence
- Sago soup
- White soup
- Steamed fish
- Fish baked in milk
- White sauce for fish
- Fried fish
- Grilled fish
- Scalloped fish
- Fricassee of chicken or rabbit
- Fricassee of sweetbread
- Fricassee of tripe
- Fricassee of brains
- Fried brains
- Grilled chop
- Savoury steak
- Scalloped beef
- Liver and bacon
- Liver and tomatoes
- Raw liver pulp
- Liver soufflé
- Liver balls
- Raw liver sandwiches
- Milk puddings and custard
- Rice and macaroni custard
- Sago or tapioca custard
- Bread and butter custard
- Queen pudding
- Sago or tapioca cream
- Baked custard
- Custard
- Caramel custard
- College pudding
- Sweet sauce
- Urney pudding
- Jam sauce
- Junket
- Baked apple
- Stewed fruits
- Dried apricots, nectarines and pears
- Dried peaches
- To stew prunes
- Jellies and creams

1953 (4th edition) identical recipes to 3rd edition

1958 (5th edition) renamed: The Southern Cookery Book. (Ross, Batchelor, Kinnear, & Crossley, 1958)
Recipes (pp 258-261)
- Lemonade
- Barley water
- Gruel
- Egg drink
- Mutton broth
- Veal broth
- Chicken broth
- Beef tea (2 recipes)
- Beef essence
- Beef tea custard
- Sago soup
- White soup
- Brown vegetable soup

Stowport Cookery Book of 500 Tested Recipes (4th edition).
(Burnie Methodist Church Trust, 1930) [Hoyle 842]
Recipes (pp50-52)
- Barley water
- Toast water
- Baked milk
- Apple water

"Welfare" Cookery Book.
(Mount Gambier Branch Mothers' and Babies' Health Association, 1930) [Hoyle 905]
Recipes (pp104-105)
- Barley water
- Beef tea
- Beef tea custard
- Boiled custard
- Chicken broth
- Egg flip
- Fricasseed brains
- Junket
- Scrambled egg
- Sago cream
- Calf's foot jelly

1931

The Blossoms Cookery Book. (Drummond, 1931) [Hoyle 458]
Recipes (pp130-132)
- Amscol milk jelly
- Nourishing Amscol milk
- Oatmeal drink
- Groats or arrowroot (for invalids)
- Nourishing custard
- Nourishing jelly
- Invalid soup
- Marmite toast
- Poached egg in Amscol milk

Cookery Book (2nd edition).
(Bundaberg Branch of the Country Women's Association, 1931) [Hoyle 320]
Recipes (pp218-219)
- Albumen water
- Barley water
- Raw beef juice
- Beef tea custard

- White wine whey
- Raw eggs
- Asparagus
- Diabetic scones

1936 (3rd edition) identical recipes
1947 (6th edition) identical recipes

The Orange Recipe Gift Book (3rd edition). (Orange District Hospital Auxiliary, 1931) [Hoyle 1011]

<u>Recipe</u> (108)
- Invalid's beef tea

1947 (4th edition) identical to 3rd edition
195-? (5th edition) identical to 3rd edition
196-? (6th edition) No invalid recipes

Between 1931 and 1936

Modern Advanced Cookery.
(The N.S.W. Cookery Teachers Association, Between 1931 and 1936) [Hoyle 984]
<u>Advice</u> (pp74-76).
[No recipes but some general cooking advice given. Descriptions of Liquid, Light, Convalescent, Special diets and Beverages for the sick: Medicinal, Nourishing and Thirst quenchers].
Rules for preparing and service food for invalids:
1. Perfect cleanliness of all utensils, enamel or earthenware for preference.
2. In cases of infectious sickness, all crockery etc should be kept apart and sterilized.
3. A feeding cup is of great assistance when giving food to a helpless patient.
4. Ingredients should be perfectly fresh and of best quality.
5. Employ the lightest cooking methods.
6. Provide as much variety as possible, but carry out doctor's orders.
7. Avoid over sweetening or strong flavours, as patient's taste is not normal.
8. Remove all traces of fat from broth of beef tea before serving.
9. Never taste food in front of the patient, or present food a second time, if once refused.
10. Serve food often, therefore it is necessary to have some food in readiness.
11. Endeavour to anticipate the patient's wishes.
12. Serve the food in small quantities and as daintily as possible – punctuality must be observed.
13. The linen should be carefully laundered.
14. Dainty china and appointments, well polished glassware and silver, play an important part in tempting the patient to partake of the food.
15. Glasses should only be filled within one inch of the top, and should be placed on a small plate.
16. A small sprig of flowers is an improvement to the appearance.
17. Always cover the tray when taking it to the patient.
18. Remove all traces of the meal as soon as possible after the patient has finished.

1948. The Advanced Commonsense Cookery Book. (The N.S.W. Public School Cookery Teachers' Association, 1948). [Hoyle 958]
Updated version of this book. Identical invalid cookery advice.

1932

Healthful Cookery. (Bartlett, 1932) [Hoyle 113]
Recipes (pp87-89)
- Marmite fondu
- Wine jelly
- Wine eggnog
- Grainut custard
- Doris cream mould
- Arrowroot gruel
- Barley water
- Marmite and milk drink
- Gluten gruel
- Granose gruel
- Eggnog
- Steamed egg
- White of egg and milk
- Bean broth
- Malted nuts and milk
- Vegetable water

1938 edition identical recipes

Some Tested Recipes. (Hughes, 1932) [Not in Hoyle]
Recipes (pp11-13)
- Barley Water for invalids (thick)
- Beef tea
- Gruel

St Luke's Cookery Book. (Higgins, 1932) [Hoyle 638]
Advice (pp198-202)
Hints on invalid cookery, points to remember in preparing food for the sick, the importance of proper diet, and general comments on cooking the following foods:
- Milk
- Eggs
- Soups
- Fish
- Jellies
- Vegetables
- Peptonised foods
- Toast
- Cutlets
- Tripe
- Brains
- Sweetbreads
- Oysters

Three types of diet are defined:

Liquid Diet consists entirely of liquid foods. In some cases of severe illness nothing but milk is given for some time, but usually beef teas, different kinds of broths, gruels, egg flips, light soups, fruit juices and cooling drinks are included in the light diet. Wines and liquors are never given unless ordered by the doctor. Tea and coffee are usually forbidden as being too stimulating. Hot milk or cocoa given at night induces sleep.

Light Diet is given in less severe illnesses or when a patient begins to improve after a severe illness. It includes anything belonging to liquid diet and in addition soft cooked eggs, omelettes, light soups, jellies, soft puddings, custards, poultry, fish and oysters, brains, sweetbreads, tender meats, also fruits and vegetables, as potatoes (mashed, creamed or roasted in their jackets, spinach, lettuce and marrow.

Convalescent Diet includes all ordinary dishes, except those difficult of digestion, as pork, veal, richer kinds of fish, cheese, pastry, and fried foods. It must be remembered that the digestive system has become weakened by illness and must not be unduly taxed.

1933

192 of the Best Recipes for Rice: The food of the people.
(Rice Marketing Board of New South Wales, 1933) [Hoyle 1140]

Recipes (pp24-25)
- Rice water
- Rice gruel
- Chicken broth
- Summer broth
- Drink for invalids
- Rice soup
- Mutton broth

The Maltovine Home Guide. (Maltovine, 1933) [Hoyle 804]

Advice (pp49-51)
[Table of the digestibility of food and information on vitamins.]

Recipes (p95)
- Raw beef tea
- Beef tea
- Mutton broth
- Chicken broth
- Toast water
- Thick barley water
- Rice water
- Stewed oysters

The Nursery Cookery Book. (The Mothercraft Association of Queensland, 1933) [Hoyle 904]

Recipes (pp106-109)
- Barley jelly
- Oat jelly
- Rice jelly
- Milk jelly
- Apple pulp
- Prune juice
- Prune pulp
- Emulsion of cod-liver oil
- Baked flour (dextrinised)
- Baked bread
- Albumen water
- Lime water
- Carrot or swede turnip juice
- Barley water
- Raw meat juice
- Whey

1934

Cookery Book (3rd edition). (Voss, 1934) [Hoyle 1332]

Recipes (pp255-265)
- Albumen water
- Apple tea
- Arrowroot pudding
- Asparagus
- Barley water
- Baked bread
- Raw beef juice
- Raw meat juice
- Beef tea custard
- Bread pudding
- Calf's or sheep's brains
- Calf's foot milk jelly
- Carrot juice
- Chicken panada

- Jelly custard
- Egg brandy
- Boiled egg
- Raw eggs
- Invalid's pudding
- Junket
- Lime water
- Oyster soup
- Oatcake
- Ground rice soufflé
- Savoury pudding
- Whey
- White wine whey
- Boiled whiting

The Popular Co-operative Cookery Book.
(Adelaide Co-operative Stores Limited, 1934) [Hoyle 10]
Advice (p41)
[General advice on invalid diet and brief description of Milk, Vegetable and Meat diets]

Recipes (pp41-42)
- Barley water
- Brain cakes
- Invalid chop
- Grilled steak or chops
- Beef tea custard
- Apple water
- Rice water

1935

Australian Cookery Book. (Eddy, 1935a) [Hoyle 468]
Advice (pp38-39)
[Description of the five usual diets: Meat, Milk, Low, Vegetable, and Ordinary]

Recipes (pp39-42)
- Beef tea custard
- Rice water
- Albumen water
- Toast water
- Baked apple
- Wine whey
- Barley water
- Invalid gruel
- Sippets
- Grilled fish
- Beef tea (3 kinds)
- Apple water
- Whey
- Eggnog or beaten egg
- Tapioca custard
- Chicken broth
- Apple delight
- Lemonade
- Light bread pudding
- Steamed batter pudding
- Prune jelly
- Tapioca cream
- Invalid chop
- Chicken cookery
- Steamed fish
- Arrowroot
- Brain cakes
- Mutton broth
- Grilled steak or chops
- Fricasseed brains
- Eggs (poached, scrambled, omelettes, steamed)

Bessie Eddy Cookery Book. (Eddy, 1935b) [Hoyle 466]
Recipes (pp54-57)

- Barley water
- Invalid gruel
- Sippets
- Grilled fish
- Beef tea (3 kinds)
- Apple water
- Whey
- Eggnog or beaten egg
- Chicken cookery
- Steamed fish
- Arrowroot
- Brain cakes
- Mutton broth
- Grilled steak or chops
- Fricasseed brains
- Eggs (poached, scrambled, omelettes, steamed)
- Tapioca custard
- Chicken broth
- Apple delight
- Light bread pudding
- Steamed batter pudding
- Lemonade
- Prune jelly
- Tapioca cream
- Invalid chop
- Beef tea custard
- Rice water
- Albumen water
- Toast water
- Baked apple
- Wine whey

Cookery Book. (Beilby, 1935) [Hoyle 152]
Advice (pp9-11).
Food for invalids should be nourishing, easily digested and it should be presented daintily.
[Classes of diets described: Ordinary (Full), Low, Milk, Light, Meat]

Recipes (pp11-12)

- Beef tea (2 methods)
- Apple water
- Chicken broth
- Egg flip
- Steamed egg

1936

The Coronation Cookery Book (1st edition). (Sawyer & Moore-Sims, 1936) [Hoyle314]
Advice (p255).
[General information on preparation and service of food for invalids]

Recipes (pp256-260)

- Beef tea (2 recipes)
- Toast water
- Sweetbreads
- Raw beef tea
- Rice water
- Treacle posset
- Barley water
- Mutton broth
- Chicken broth
- Calf's foot jelly
- Lamb in jelly
- Eggs baked in tomato

- Egg jelly
- Blackcurrant tea
- Broiled chicken
- Boiled lettuce
- Apple glace
- Fish cream
- Veal broth
- Barley cream soup
- Egg wine
- Lemon rice pudding
- Fish quenelles
- Albumen water
- Egg flip
- Chicken shape
- A pick-me-up for invalids
- Bread jelly (can be used for infants)
- Milk jelly
- Steamed whiting
- Steamed bream
- Marshmallow custard
- Creamed fish
- Invalid chop
- Beef jelly

1938 (2nd edition) identical recipes
1941 (3rd edition) identical recipes
1945 (4th edition) identical recipes
1954 (7th edition) identical recipes
1978 (14th edition) identical recipes – <u>without</u> treacle posset, egg-jelly; <u>plus</u> steamed eggs, lemon foam

Delicious Milk Dishes and Drinks. (Milk Board Melbourne, 1936) [Hoyle 859]
<u>Recipes</u> (pp18-22)

- Barley cream
- Milk soup for invalids
- Milk and tomato savoury
- Savoury cup custard
- Invalid pick-me-up
- A tripe dainty
- Moulded chicken
- Nutritious junket
- Prune custard
- Calf's foot jelly
- Invalid dish
- Brains a la appetite
- Ovaltine junket
- Apple blancmange
- Poached snowballs
- Milk jelly with orange sauce
- Quaker oats with milk
- Snow eggs with custard
- Quaker oats with egg

It's in Your Kitchen: Simple remedies and hints for everyone. (Parry, 1936) [Not in Hoyle]
[Author was a nursing sister and lecturer for the St John's Ambulance Association]
<u>Advice</u> (pp17-18)
[General advice meal service for the sick]

<u>Recipes</u> (page numbers in brackets)

- Barley water (60)
- "Imperial drink" (75)
- Albumen water (78)
- Egg junket (78)
- Lightly cooked egg (79)
- Egg-milk stout (79)
- Oatmeal gruel (88)
- Arrowroot gruel (88)

- Barley gruel (89)
- Linseed tea (100)
- Raw meat juice (103)
- Beef tea (104)
- Milk (106)
- Junket (109)
- Milk jelly (109)
- Milk bread (110)
- Oatmeal (114)
- Orange juice (118)
- Orange and grapefruit cocktail (119)
- Orange snow (119)
- Milk tea (137)
- Tomato juice (139)
- Tomato soup (140)

1937

"Bethany" Cookery Book. (Bethany Babies Home, 1937) [Hoyle 158]

Advice (p59)

[General advice and description of 4 types of diet (Low, Milk, Vegetable, and Meat)]

Recipes (pp59-63)

- Beef tea (2 recipes)
- Albuminised milk (2 recipes)
- Barley water (2 recipes)
- Bran tea
- Coffee custard
- Apple water
- Eggnog
- Fruit whip
- Lemon whey
- Linseed tea
- Sherry whey (for fever)
- Mutton broth
- Port wine jelly
- Rice water
- Sago jelly
- Junket (2 recipes)
- Coffee junket
- Steamed custard
- Gruel
- Egg jelly
- Jellied beef tea
- Whey and wine jelly

Domestic Science Handbook (NSW) (3rd edition).
(New South Wales Cookery Teachers Association, 1937) [Hoyle 399]

Advice (pp31-32)

7 days of menus for a convalescent diet including the following dishes (names only, no recipes):

- Wholemeal porridge
- Mutton broth
- Grilled chop and mashed potatoes, spinach
- Steamed cup pudding
- Oatmeal gruel
- Poached egg
- White soup
- Baked mutton and baked potatoes, pumpkin, peas
- Semolina pudding
- Tomatoes on toast
- Bread and milk
- Fried sweetbreads
- Lentil soup
- Boiled fish and boiled potatoes and beans
- Junket and prunes
- Veal broth
- Fricassee of tripe

- Brain cakes
- Boiled fowl, bread sauce
- Chicken broth
- Queen pudding
- Chicken salad
- Lettuce and nut salad
- *Plus*: bread, butter, fruits

1939 (5th edition) identical menus

194-? A Handbook of Home Management.
(The Department of Education Victoria, 194-?) [Hoyle 410]
Identical content to NSW handbook.

Milk Recipes for Young and Old.
(Betterment and Publicity Board Victorian Railways, 1937) [Hoyle 864]
Recipes (p19)
- Bread and milk
- Milk toast
- Gruel
- Albuminised milk

1938

Diets: Eating for health. (Flay, 1938) [Hoyle 647]
Advice (p34)
[General information on serving meals for the invalid]

Recipes (pp34-36)
- Egg flip
- Eggs – poached, steamed, coddles, scrambled, baked
- Chicken broth
- Invalid's broth

Domestic Science Handbook. (Department of Education Victoria, 1938) [Hoyle 408]
Advice (pp29-30)
General advice (foods for convalescents need to be nourishing to build up the body and repair waste due to illness; foods rich in protein must be served at each meal) and 7 days of menus for a convalescent diet, including the following dishes (names only, no recipes):
- Wholewheat porridge
- Wheatmeal bread
- Mutton broth
- Grilled chop
- Mashed potatoes
- Spinach
- Steamed cup pudding
- Bread
- Jelly
- Stewed fruit
- Oatmeal gruel
- Poached egg
- White soup
- Baked mutton
- Potatoes in jackets
- Pumpkin
- Peas
- Semolina pudding
- Fried sweetbread
- Lentil soup
- Boiled fish
- Beans
- Junket
- Prunes

- Veal broth
- Fricassee of tripe
- Beans
- Steamed custard
- Wholemeal cake
- Oatmeal porridge
- Brain cakes
- Apple cake
- Lettuce and nut salad
- Fricassee of brains
- Baked apple
- Pea soup
- Baked pumpkin
- Cauliflower and sauce
- Queen pudding
- Chicken salad
- Fresh pineapple

1940 (6th edition) (Department of Education Victoria, 1940) [Hoyle 410]
[New article on the science of nutrition. Same menus as 1938 but additional general advice]:
To balance the diet fresh fruits and vegetables must be eaten; skins included for roughage; some citrus fruits daily

No liquids with meals

Two glasses of lemon drink or orangeade up to one hour before meals.

1941 (7th edition) identical to 6th edition
1942 (8th edition) identical to 6th edition
1948? (9th edition) identical to 6th edition

Between 1938 and 1940

For Invalids and Convalescents.
(Davis Gelatine Cookery Department, Between 1938 and 1940) [Not in Hoyle]
<u>Advice</u> (pp1-2)

Preparing meals for the invalid and convalescent is ever a delicate task and the housewife who has a patient to care for finds gelatine indispensable. Food prepared with gelatine has all the essentials, which the invalid dietary requires. It is nourishing, easily digested, can be made so very attractive that it whets the feeble and indifferent appetite, and can be flavoured so delicately that the sensitive palate is pleased and the flow of the digestive juices is stimulated.

It is generally admitted that food for invalids and convalescents is nourishing and usually easily digested, but very often unattractive and the flavour not very appetising. The importance of appearance is often overlooked and yet this factor decides many times whether the patient will have a normal desire for sustenance, or, because of the unappetizing look of the food, be indifferent to it.

In combination with milk, gelatine is particularly beneficial, and milk plays an important part of the invalid dietary. Gelatine possesses the power to keep the curds of milk in a small and finely divided stated; it has also the power to emulsify the milk fats into tiny droplets. When curds are small and fluffy and the fat in tiny globules, the milk is readily acted upon by the digestive juices and changed into the form in which the body absorbs it. In addition to its effect upon the curd and fat of milk, gelatine has other properties which aid the digestion, for it has the advantage of fixing, i.e. rendering non-active a good deal of the acid in the process of digestion.

<u>Recipes</u> (pp2-7)
- Orange jelly
- Orange whip
- Orange sponge
- Orange Bavarian
- Orange cream
- Orange & honey cream
- Lemon cream
- Jellied chicken
- Jellied beef tea
- Prune jelly
- Asparagus cream
- Wine jelly (2 recipes)
- Jellied soup
- Egg jelly
- Wine whey jelly
- Snow dessert
- Simple Cream
- Pineapple Bavarian
- Milk jelly
- Coffee jelly
- Cocoa jelly

196-? Ulcer Diets & Recipes for Convalescents.
  (Davis Gelatine Department of Home Economics, 196-?)
Identical recipes.

The Leader Spare Corner Book Parts 10, 11, 12: A unique collection of home and household hints & kitchen recipes. (Anon, Between 1938 and 1940) [Hoyle 776]
<u>Recipes</u> (pp30-31)
- Beef tea
- Mutton broth
- Barley milk soup
- Puree of beef
- Meat jelly
- Fish custard
- Fish cream
- Steamed chop
- Stewed sweetbread
- Apple cream
- Egg jelly
- Prune soufflé

1939

Good Health: Cookery book and food manual. (Harris, 1939) [Hoyle 625]
<u>Recipes</u> (pp65-66)
- Invalid's egg
- Beef tea
- Stonycrest pudding
- Special mutton cutlet
- Chicken for an invalid
- Sweetbread for an invalid

1940 edition identical recipes

1940-1950

Homecraft Book: A work compiled for the home lover (Victorian Association of Creches, 1941)

The Kitchen Front (Australian Broadcasting Commission, 1943)

194-?

Dainty Dishes: A book of selected recipes by Nestlé. (Nestlé, 194-?) [Hoyle 935]
Recipes (p23)
- Biscuits or rusks with Lactogen
- Cereal pudding with Lactogen
- Baked custard
- Ground rice custard

The Golden Cookery Book: With invaluable household recipes, invalid cookery, etc. (Anon, 194-?-a) [Hoyle 575]
Recipes (pp109-117)
- Beef tea
- Meat juice
- Egg flip
- Egg jelly
- Meat jelly
- Oatmeal jelly
- Oatmeal gruel
- Invalid's pudding
- Fish for an invalid
- Poached egg in milk ("this is the most nourishing way of preparing eggs for invalids")
- To boil an egg
- Toast
- Arrowroot, made with milk
- Arrowroot, made with water
- Milk toast
- Broth for an invalid
- Mutton broth
- Invalid custard
- Custard savoury
- Tripe ("very digestible and very nourishing")
- Sheep's brains
- To grill a joint of chicken
- Chicken broth
- Steamed fish
- Chop
- Oatmeal water
- Linseed tea
- Rice water
- Beef tea and oatmeal
- Lemonade
- Bran tea
- Barley water (2 recipes)
- Egg lemonade
- Egg drink
- Soda, milk and egg
- Apple water (2 recipes)
- Rhubarb water
- Blackcurrant drink ("very good in affections of the throat, and when feverish")
- Hot lemonade
- Pineapple lemonade
- Prune water
- Toast water
- To sterilise milk

The Mallee Cookery Book. (Berri Methodist Ladies Guild, 194-?) [Not in Hoyle]
Recipes (p37)
- Mutton broth
- Gruel
- Puffed egg
- Albumen water
- Beef tea

The Milky Way of Cookery: 73 Trufood recipes. (Anon, 194-?-b) [Not in Hoyle]
Recipe (p28)
- Invalid cup

Notes and Recipes on Invalid Cookery and Nutrition. (Giles & Rapley, 194-?) [Not in Hoyle]
[A book from the Emily McPherson College for student nurses]
Advice (pp1-5)
[Includes care of stoves, kitchen cleanliness and purchasing, food economics, essentials of a normal diet and some general rules for a nurse when serving meals]

Recipes (pp6-45)
- Blancmange
- Chocolate blancmange
- Bread and milk
- Rice baked in milk
- Gruel
- Porridge
- Arrowroot
- Boiled rice
- Boiled sago
- Junket
- Lemon whey
- Albumenised milk
- Jellied milk
- Stewed tripe
- Fricasseed veal, rabbit or chops
- Fricasseed brains
- Calves' or sheep's brains on toast
- Stewed sweetbreads
- Boiled mutton
- Steamed chops
- Grilled chops
- Grilled steak
- Beefsteak balls
- Raw beef sandwiches
- Brains and bacon
- Grilled chicken with bacon
- Steamed or boiled chicken with sauce
- Roast chicken
- Creamed chicken or ramekins
- Casserole of liver
- Liver and bacon
- Liver juice
- Liver in tomatoes
- Liver tomato soup
- Liver cocktail
- Liver and spaghetti
- Liver sandwiches
- Grilled liver
- Steamed fish
- Raw oysters
- Boiled fish
- Baked fish
- Scalloped fish
- Grilled fish
- Boiled eggs
- Buttered eggs
- Swiss egg
- Shirred egg
- Poached egg
- Scrambled egg
- Sweet omelette
- Savoury omelette
- Egg flip
- Custard sauce
- Banana or fruit custard
- Fruit trifle
- Cup or steamed custard
- Caramel custard
- Grain custard
- Baked custard
- Bread and butter custard

- Steamed pudding
- Cabbage
- Spinach and silver beet
- French beans
- Green peas
- Marrow
- Pumpkin
- Carrots and parsnips
- Potatoes
- Artichokes or turnips
- Asparagus
- Brussels sprouts
- Baked onions in milk
- Cauliflower
- Potato salad
- Lettuce salad
- Haricot bean salad
- Cold vegetable salad
- Salmon salad
- Fruit salad
- Carrot and liver salad
- Apple salad
- Salad dressing (2 recipes)
- French dressing
- Cooked salad dressing
- Compote of fruit
- Baked apple
- Apple snow
- Fruit fool
- Lemon or fruit jelly
- Wine jelly
- Fruit in jelly
- Fruit flummery
- Baked orange or lemon pudding
- Fruit fluff
- Mutton broth
- Gravy broth
- Chicken broth
- Clear vegetable soup
- Sago cream soup
- Tomato soup
- Celery milk soup
- Oyster soup
- Beef tea
- Raw beef tea
- Beef juice
- Lemonade
- Fruit drink
- Tea
- Coffee
- Cocoa
- Albumen or egg water
- Barley water (2 recipes)
- Toast water
- Sweet white sauce
- Egg sauce
- Anchovy sauce
- Parsley sauce
- Caper sauce
- Onion sauce
- Brain sauce
- Cheese sauce
- Lemon sauce
- Tomato sauce
- Jam sauce
- Sweet lemon sauce
- Maitre d'hotel butter

An Outline of Cookery. (Red Cross Emergency Service, 194-?) [Not in Hoyle]
<u>Recipes</u> (pp16-30)
- Gruel
- Porridge
- Arrowroot
- Blancmange
- Chocolate blancmange
- Bread and milk
- Boiled rice (plain)
- Boiled sago (plain)
- Baked rice
- Baked custard

- Steamed custard
- Grain custard
- Lemon jelly
- Fruit in jelly
- Compote of fruit
- Baked apple
- Apple snow
- Fruit fool
- Fricasseed tripe
- Fricasseed veal
- Fricasseed brains
- Grilled chop
- Beef steak balls
- Liver puree
- Chicken for invalids
- Steamed whiting
- Grilled whiting
- Baked flathead
- Boiled bream
- Raw oysters
- Foundation sauce
- Egg sauce
- Fish stock
- Oyster soup
- Mutton broth
- Beef tea
- Raw beef tea
- Beef juice
- Sago cream soup
- Tomato cream soup
- Barley water
- Egg flip
- Eggnog
- Albumen or egg water
- Junket
- Poached egg
- Lemonade

Recipes for Use in Home Science Classes (9th revised edition). (Blackmore, 194-?) [Hoyle 164]
Recipes (pp56-62)
- Arrowroot or cornflour
- Apple snow
- Barley water
- Beef tea
- Bread and milk
- Egg flip
- Egg (steamed)
- Fish (steamed)
- Gruel or porridge
- Lemon snow
- Lemonade
- Mock cream
- Orange jelly
- Sago soup
- Savoury custard
- Spanish cream
- Salad dressing (unboiled)
- French dressing
- Various salads

Robinson's Cookery Book. (Naylor, 194-?) [Hoyle 933]
Recipes (pp34-36)
- Gruel
- Rice water
- Beef tea
- Barley water (2 recipes)
- Oatmeal drinks

1940

Australian Cookery of Today Illustrated. (Prudence, 1940) [Hoyle 1108]
Advice (pp49-50)
[General advice on invalid and special diets. Also includes one week's menu (p51), information on raw liver diet (p55), and information on fat free diet (p56)]

Recipes (pp50-57)
- Beef tea
- Gruel
- Oat flake soup
- Cold milk dish
- Rice pudding (sweet or savoury)
- Egg jelly
- White of egg cake
- Fig drink
- Brains or sweetbread with asparagus
- Egg snow
- Cup custard
- Apple snow
- Chicken ragout
- Minced veal omelette
- Whiting with spinach
- Fruit brulé
- Oatmeal biscuits
- Chicken for a convalescent
- Steamed chicken
- Chicken rissoles
- Poultry pudding
- Chicken custard
- Chicken broth
- Liver cocktail
- Savoury minced liver
- Liver in claret
- Liver and mushroom rissoles
- Liver relish
- Liver cakes
- Sweet dish with liver
- Stuffed tomatoes
- Liver pudding
- Claret with steamed liver
- Liver slices
- Vegetable stock
- Rice soup
- Fish soup
- Steamed chicken with vegetables
- Tomato soup with sago
- Fish in jelly
- Fish cooked in paper
- Veal stew
- Substitute sauce (without butter fat)
- Salad dressing (without oil)
- Fruit jelly

The Better Housekeeping Bureau Cook Book. (Irwin & Fox, 1940) [Hoyle 682]
Advice (p109)
[General information on invalid diet]

Recipes (pp109-110)
- Junket
- Beef tea
- Barley water
- Egg flip
- Gruel
- Soda-water and milk
- Fruit junket

Suggested Light Meals (pp110-111)
- Cream of chicken soup, brown bread and butter or toast, fruit jelly with sponge fingers.
- Lightly poached egg on spinach with buttered toast, junket with stewed apples or prunes.
- Small fillet of sole (baked or fried), with cream sauce. Vermicelli pudding.
- Scrambled egg and tomato on toast. Sponge roll and cream.
- Savoury omelet with parsley and ham, brown bread and butter, custard and stewed fruit, biscuits and cream cheese.
- Lamb cutlet grilled with potato croquette and braised onion or buttered carrots. Ripe fruit with cream or junket.
- Cheese soufflé baked in individual dishes, tomato salad, tapioca or rice pudding with jam or jelly.

Calling All Cooks! (1st edition). (Newman, 1940) [Hoyle 987]

Advice (pp245-247)

Beverages are an important item in invalid cookery. In acute illness they often form the only medium by which any nourishment can be taken at all, and as a means of quenching thirst they are particularly useful at every stage of illness. Beverages may be divided into three classes:
1. Refreshing (including lemonade, fruit drinks, aerated water)
2. Nourishing (beverages containing nourishing ingredients such as milk, eggs, soups and broths)
3. Stimulating (tea, coffee, beef tea and various patent essences and juices which, though they do not actually build up the body, are invaluable as a tonic to weakened energies and nerves).

Recipes (pp248-278)
- Fish custard
- Fish stewed in milk
- Fish soufflé (baked)
- Fricassee of oysters
- Steamed fish
- A restorative soup
- Mutton broth
- Chicken broth
- Stewed ox tail
- Celery and rice soup
- Cream of barley
- Sago cream soup
- Creamed liver
- Mutton quenelles
- Fricasseed brains
- Beef creams
- Chicken and macaroni timbales
- Boiled pigeon
- Creamed chicken
- Tripe and onions
- Snow-capped apples
- Banana cream
- Apple cream
- Buttered apples
- Lemon sponge
- Meringued peaches
- Custard pie
- Castle puddings
- Prune soufflé
- Stewed fruits
- Baked apple custard
- Apple and tapioca pudding

- Pineapple and cornflour meringue
- Caramel rice pudding
- Thin custard
- Caramel custard
- Junket
- Spanish cream
- Tapioca cream
- A delicate bread pudding
- Hasty pudding
- Queen pudding
- Sweet omelette
- Egg jelly
- Milk jelly
- Wine jelly
- Root vegetables
- Green vegetables
- Mashed potatoes
- Toast water
- Treacle posset (for a cold)
- Rum and milk
- Rice water
- Milk gruel
- Lemonade
- Egg and rum
- Egg flip
- Albuminised milk or water
- Cocoa
- Coffee or tea with an egg
- To make coffee
- Brandy and egg mixture
- Bran tea (a remedy for hoarseness)
- Blackcurrant drink
- Apple water
- Linseed tea

1944 (3rd edition) identical recipes
1949 (5th edition) identical recipes

Cookery for Invalids Convalescents and Children. (Kirkhope, 1940, 1944) [Hoyle 721]

Advice (pp1-8)
[General advice on nutrition and food groups (including guides to boil or steam root and green vegetables) and diet types]

Recipes (pp9-49)
- Boiled eggs
- Poached eggs
- Eggnog
- Scrambled egg
- Boiled custard
- Baked custard
- Baked apple
- Caramel custard
- Sweet omelette
- Savoury omelette
- Cocoa
- Coffee junket
- Junket
- Caramel
- Caramel junket
- Fruit junket
- Simple cream
- Wine jelly
- Blancmange
- Banana custard
- Boiled bream, schnapper, cod etc
- Fried filleted fish
- Fried garfish
- Fish cakes
- Fish pie
- Baked flathead
- Steamed whiting with lemon sauce
- Fish stock
- Fish scallop
- Fried flounder
- Meat stock
- Mutton broth
- Chicken broth
- Tomato soup

- Oyster soup
- Beef tea (2 recipes)
- Jellied beef tea
- Cream soups
- Baked stuffed potato
- Rice baked in milk
- Bread and butter pudding
- Grain custard (rice, sago, tapioca)
- Queen pudding
- Cocoanut custard
- Cabinet pudding
- Foundation steamed pudding
- Apple cream
- Compote fruit
- Orange foam
- Barley water
- Lemonade
- Lemon egg jelly
- Toast water
- Mutton cutlets
- Lettuce salad
- Tomato salad
- Potato salad
- Haricot bean salad
- Beetroot salad
- Cold vegetable salad
- Salad dressing (2 recipes)
- French dressing
- French salad
- Savoury butter
- Grilled whiting
- Stewed tripe
- Fricasseed brains
- Foundation white sauce
- Brown sauce
- Tomato sauce
- Creamota porridge
- Creamota gruel
- Creamota wafers
- A most nourishing drink for convalescents
- Black coffee

1944 (2nd edition). (Kirkhope, 1944) [Hoyle 722]
Identical recipes plus:
- Albuminised milk
- Roast chicken
- Veal forcemeat
- Boiled fowl
- Steamed fowl
- Grilled spatchcock

Household Book. (Victorian Children's Aid Society Home, 1940) [Hoyle 222]
Advice (pp30-31)
[No recipes; an alphabet of foods possessing definite medicinal value, e.g.]
- Apples for remedying indigestion and cleansing the system and teeth
- Barley for reducing temperatures and purifying the kidneys
- Carrots of anaemia and the nerves…

1941

The CWA Cookery Book and Household Hints (5th edition). (Barnes, 1941) [Hoyle 338]
Recipes (pp342-346)
- Beef tea
- Chicken broth
- Mutton broth
- Strengthening broth
- Beef tea custard
- Filleted fish
- Apple soufflé
- Arrowroot jelly

- Milk gruel
- Lemon albumen
- Barley water (2 recipes)
- Boiled milk with suet
- Egg flip
- Linseed tea
- Toast water
- Raw beef juice
- Lemon whey
- Sherry whey
- Whey

1986 (38th edition) (Barnes, 1986)
Recipes (pp337-340)
- Apple soufflé
- Arrowroot jelly
- Barley water
- Beef tea
- Beef tea custard
- Chicken broth
- Egg flip
- Lemon whey
- Mutton broth
- Olive oil tonic
- Raw beef juice
- Raw liver juice
- Raw liver sandwiches
- Seamed fish
- Strengthening broth
- Whey

Homecraft Book: A work compiled for the home lover.
(Victorian Association of Creches, 1941)[Hoyle 1326]
Advice (pp23-24)
[General advice on invalid cookery, with almost identical wording for that in The "Lifeguard" Cookery Book (Drake, 1922), including]:
A woman may be excused if she cannot make a cake, but it should be regarded as a social crime if she is not able to prepare a good cup of beef tea, or nourishing soup, and a few simple dishes which will help and not retard an invalid's recovery. Concerning the service of foods to invalids, the following points are important:
- Give small quantities at short intervals
- Try and anticipate the patient's wants, and recollect that thirst is nearly always present on waking; therefore have a drink ready, so that the patient need not ask for it
- Never ask invalids what they would like to eat, unless you have noticed their enjoyment of a certain dish, then it may be suggested that they have it again
- Avoid all possible risk of smell of cooking entering the sick room
- Serve rather less, than more, than the patient will probably require
- A small whole jelly or pudding or custard is preferable to serving from a larger one
- Remove all trace of the meal from the sick room
- Never serve "warmed up" food. Everything (with the exceptions of broths) should be freshly cooked.

Recipes (pp24-28)
- Beef tea (2 recipes)
- Raw beef tea
- Clear barley water
- Barley water (thick)
- Marrow sandwiches or marrow on toast
- Toast water
- Albumen water
- Egg jelly

- Gruel
- Eggs
- Butter egg
- Fried oysters
- Pigs in blankets
- Oysters
- Scalloped oysters
- Invalid grilled fish
- Raw beef rolls
- Beef tea jelly
- "Egg bouillon"
- Mutton or chicken broth
- A delightful fish soup
- Sheep's trotters stewed
- Stewed tripe
- Calves' or sheep's brains on toast
- Cup custard
- Arrowroot
- Savoury omelette
- Light bread pudding
- Egg flip
- Stewed chop and rice
- Brains and sauce
- Brain canapés
- Apple water
- Chicken cutlets
- Egg brandy

1942

Adelect Invalid and Convalescent Cookery. (Benson, 1942) [Hoyle 17]

Advice (pp3-8)
[General information on home nursing, types of diets and general rules for invalid feeding. Best vegetables for invalids (p25): potatoes mashed, French beans, peas, spinach, cauliflower, and trombone. General advice on cooking of meat, fish and poultry.]

Recipes (pp9-41)
- Barley water (2 recipes)
- Lemonade
- Egg flip
- Whey
- Apple water
- Treacle posset (induces sweating)
- Toast water
- Gruel
- White stock
- Brown stock
- Fish stock
- Mutton broth
- Sago cream soup
- Tomato soup
- Beef tea (2 recipes)
- Raw beef tea
- Beef tea custard
- Steamed fish
- Sauce for fish
- Fish baked in milk
- Grilled fish
- Fricassee of sweetbreads
- Fricassee of tripe
- Fricassee of brains
- Minced liver
- Fried liver and bacon
- Crumbed brains
- Poached egg
- Scrambled egg
- Steamed egg
- Plain omelette
- Puffed omelette
- Plain custard
- Cup of arrowroot cornflour or groats
- Sago cream
- Bread and butter custard
- Cereal custard
- Junket

- Blancmange
- Steamed college pudding
- Cornflour sauce
- Jam sauce
- Stewed fruit
- Baked apples or pears
- Lemon or orange jelly
- Milk jelly
- Spanish cream
- Sponge cake
- Paris creams
- Swiss roll
- Honey sandwich cake
- Plain cake

Cookery: A short course for beginners. (Education Department of Victoria, 1942) [Hoyle 1323]
Recipes (pp8-43)
Those noted in the text as useful for invalids are:
- Gruel
- Bread and milk
- Blancmange
- Soft-boiled egg
- Scrambled egg on toast
- Poached egg on toast
- Junket
- Broth
- Beef tea
- White stew
- Boiled custard

Over 100 Ways of Using Bread. (NSW Bread Industry, 1942) [Hoyle 179]
Recipes (pp27-29)
- Liver soufflé
- Chicken and egg broth
- Stewed sweetbreads
- Fish quenelles
- Cheese custard
- Mince chop
- Egg pudding
- Orange pudding
- Toast water
- Fairy fingers
- Bread cutlets
- Dumpling

1943

The Kitchen Front. (Australian Broadcasting Commission, 1943) [Hoyle 59]
[Selections of talks from the spokesman of the ABC's Nutrition Advisory Committee]
Advice (pp35-36)
Chapter on Meals for the Convalescent includes:
- Stimulating the appetite comes first. Broths, beef teas and soups are permitted, and although their actual food value is very low, they are important in being able to stimulate the flow of gastric juices so that a desire for food is created.
- The food should be light and easily digested, yet nourishing. For breakfast eggs, tomatoes and fish can be served. A mid-morning glass of milk or fruit juice is good and an egg-flip if tolerated is better still. For luncheon: soups, grilled fish, brains, grilled chops, underdone minute steak and red and green vegetables can be given.

- Light desserts of eggs, milk, cream, gelatine, and fruit pulp or juice are valuable, served as orange, apricot or passionfruit soufflés, Bavarian creams or Devonshire junkets.
- Fricassees, cream soups and milk desserts all help the daily intake of milk. These dishes are delicious for an evening meal. Veal or chicken fricassee, creamed chicken pie, fish omelettes, egg mayonnaise, cauliflower cheese and other cheese dishes are all easily digested and appetising, as well as nourishing.

"Truth" and "Daily Mirror" Cookery Book (1st edition). (Anon, 1943) [Hoyle 1307]
Advice (p156)
Invalid cookery is a branch all on its own and often even the experienced cook is at a loss to know what to serve and how to prepare dishes that are light, nourishing and tempting. Diabetic diet, of course, is under medical supervision. The selected recipes, however, may solve the problem of variation in these restricted menus.

Recipes (pp156-163)
- Sherry arrowroot
- Barley water
- Apple barley water
- Invalid beef tea
- Chicken cream
- Teacup custard pudding
- Beef tea with egg
- Milk and suet
- Coddle egg
- Egg flip
- Gruel
- Apple snow
- Liver for invalids
- Minced liver
- Steamed sole
- Egg jelly
- Spinach soufflé
- Port wine jelly
- Baked apple meringue
- Invalid's Christmas pudding
- Asparagus soup
- Salmon scramble
- Diabetic biscuits
- Almond sponge
- Sugarless cake
- Bran cakes
- Biscuits
- Bread
- Bran muffins
- Good nutloaf

1936 (3rd edition) identical recipes

1944

Cookery Book: Over 500 tested recipes.
(Country Women's Association Queensland - Nambour Branch, 1944) [Hoyle 322]
Recipes (pp101-103)
- Minced tripe
- Custard
- Barley water
- Whey
- Steamed fish
- Coddled egg
- Steamed egg
- Beef tea

The "Victory" Cookery Book. (Jackson, 1944) [Hoyle 688]
Recipes (pp165-166)
- Delicious egg jelly
- Lemon snow pudding
- Brains on toast
- Orange egg flip
- Mild flavoured vegetables
- Whole cereals
- Lemon egg jelly
- Variety of cuts for invalid from 1 chicken or fowl
- Fluffed egg
- All ripe fruits

1945

The Beefine Way: A range of tested recipes. (Anon, 1945a) [Not in Hoyle]
Advice (p3)
Beefine is prepared from choice beef and contains a high percentage of peptones and other nitrogenous compounds. Beefine makes finest beef tea but it is also an excellent flavouring for soups, stews, curries, pies etc. … Proved for invalids, praised by athletes, satisfying and sustaining for the aged, ideal for brain-workers, invaluable for convalescents, affords relief to sufferers from indigestion and nerves. Also tones up the system. Beefine enriches the blood, is appetising, delicious, refreshing and wholesome. Beefine is served regularly in hospitals and leading institutions and is highly recommended – preferred because it is peptonised.

Recipes (pp4, 9)
- Beefine tonic wine (2 recipes)
- Beefine and milk
- Beefine egg flip
- Topic appetiser
- Pick-me-up
- Beefine broth
- Invalid beef tea custard
- Beefine soup for convalescents
- Beefine jelly

The Victorian Country Women's Recipe Book 1945-1946. (Anon, 1945b) [Hoyle 1328]
Advice (pp42-44)
The following points are important:
1. Food should be served in small quantities, absolutely clean, and with as appetising an appearance as possible.
2. In most cases it should be served when cooked and not allowed to stand too long or it will lose its freshness.
3. As a rule, the dish should not be served a second or consecutive time.
4. Only the very freshest and best of fish, milk, meat and eggs should be used.
5. All seasonings should be very moderate.
6. All food, whether hot or cold, should be sent from the kitchen covered.
7. The invalid should not be consulted as to what he desires; each tray is then somewhat of a surprise.
8. Everything suggestive of medicine should be banished while food is set before the invalid.
9. Tray should be bright, silver or cruet clean, glass sparkling, serviettes spotless and fresh flowers from garden may be added.

Recipes (pp44-47)
- Beef tea
- Barley water (2 recipes)
- Cup custard
- Arrowroot
- Savoury omelette
- Light bread pudding
- Mutton broth
- Albumen water
- Toast water
- Apple water
- Beef tea custard
- Egg flip
- Stewed chop and rice
- Brains and sauce
- Brain canapés
- Chicken broth
- Chicken cutlets
- Egg broth
- Egg brandy
- Fried brains
- Stewed sweetbreads
- Tripe
- Oatmeal gruel
- Pineapple sponge

1950 (Revised edition) identical advice

Wartime Cookery. (Dunne, 1945) [Hoyle 459]
Advice (pp5-6)
[Short section on tempting the appetite]

Recipe (p5)
- Baked egg

1946

Elementary Text Book of Cookery, Laundry and Home Management. (The New South Wales Public School Cookery Teachers' Association, 1946) [Not in Hoyle]
Advice (p13)
Information invalid cookery includes the following rules:
1. Obtain a diet sheet.
2. Observe perfect cleanliness.
3. Use fresh ingredients of the best quality.
4. Cook foods by the lightest methods, viz, steaming, grilling, boiling.
5. If the patient is feverish, serve liquid foods only.
6. Provide variety to stimulate appetite.
7. Always have some food, such as broth, soup or fruit drink, in readiness. Note: Barley water should be freshly made every 12 hours unless kept in a refrigerator.

1947

The Kuitpo Cookery Book (6th edition). (Anon, 1947) [Hoyle 749]

<u>Advice</u> (p105)

Description on Fluid, Light and Special Diets.

- *Fluid*: milk, albumen water, barley water, milk and soda, orange and lemon drinks, tea, coffee and cocoa. Sometimes broths, junket and egg-flips, ice cream
- *Light*: broths, milk puddings, egg-flip, ice cream, brains, tripe or fish (steamed or boiled with milk), eggs, jellies, fruit pieces, thin bread and butter, plain biscuits, sponge cake.

Description of the Hay System and sample weekly menu (pp109-112) [A system of eating based on thorough mastication and avoiding consumption of starchy or sweet foods with protein foods]

<u>Recipes</u> (pp105-109)

- Albumen water
- Egg flip
- Hot milk and soda-water
- White wine whey
- Whey
- Raw meat juice
- Eggnog
- White of egg and milk
- Orange drink
- Barley water (2 recipes)
- Barley water – lemon drink
- Beef tea (2 recipes)
- Invalid soup
- Chicken broth
- Mutton broth
- Milk jelly
- Egg poached in milk
- Fish in milk
- Fricasseed brains
- Milk jelly (2 recipes)
- Sago jelly mould
- Fruit jellies

1948

The Book of Good Housekeeping: Compiled by the Good Housekeeping Institute (First Australian edition). (Good Housekeeping Institute, 1948) [Hoyle 582]

[Original English edition first published 1944]

<u>Advice</u> (pp430-433)

[General information on catering for the invalid]

<u>Recipes</u> (pp433-438)

- Barley water
- Egg flip
- Lemon water
- Apple water
- Cream of tomato soup
- Grated carrot soup
- Cheese moulds
- Cold fish soufflé
- Chicken mousse
- Coffee creams
- Mock cream
- Butterscotch mould
- Orange mould
- Semolina whip
- Baked semolina soufflé
- Apple or apricot meringue
- Omelette soufflé
- Lime milk jelly
- Blackcurrant whip
- Egg junket

- Baked custard pudding
- Crème caramel
- French chocolate custard

Manual of Home Economics: In 4 sections comprising cookery theory, food study, laundry work and home management (1st edition). (Cullen, 1948) [Not in Hoyle}

<u>Advice</u> (pp112-114)
[General advice on diets in sickness and foods suitable for Liquid, Soft and Light Diets]

1949

Invalid Cookery: A text book for hospital trainees. (Missingham, 1949) [Hoyle 872]

<u>Advice</u> (pp9-28)
[General nutrition information and advice on serving foods, tray setting and storage]

<u>Recipe</u> (pp29-72)
- Apple Charlotte
- Apple snow
- Bacon grilled
- Bananas baked
- Barley water
- Beef steak balls
- Beef tea
- Benger's food
- Brains fricassee
- Brains fried
- Bread and butter custard
- Bread sauce
- Canary pudding
- Carrots
- Cauliflower
- Chicken broth
- Chicken boiled
- Chicken steamed
- Chicken baked
- Chicken stewed
- Chicken roast
- Chicken jellied
- Chop grilled
- Coffee rolls
- Coffee
- Cocoa
- Cornflour biscuits
- Cornflour mould
- Currant water
- Custard crumb
- Custard soft
- Custard baked
- Custard caramel
- Custard egg and cornflour
- Custard & fresh fruit
- Egg baked
- Egg coddles
- Egg flip cold
- Egg flip hot
- Egg hard cooked
- Egg in bread sauce
- Egg nests
- Eggnog
- Egg omelette
- Egg poached
- Egg steamed
- Egg soft cooked
- Egg scrambled
- Fish fried
- Fish grilled
- Fish steamed
- Fish stock
- Fruit juice
- Fruit punch
- Jam sauce
- Junket

- Lamb stewed
- Lemonade
- Lemon baked
- Lemon pudding
- Lemon snow
- Lemon squash
- Liver casserole
- Liver cocktail
- Liver grilled
- Liver juice
- Liver mould
- Meringue
- Meringue apples
- Milk albumenised
- Milk bouillon
- Milk jelly
- Milk malted
- Milk posset
- Milk punch
- Milk puddings
- Mutton broth
- Nectarines baked
- Onions
- Oranges baked
- Orange jelly
- Orangeade
- Oysters fricassee
- Patty cakes
- Pears baked
- Peaches baked
- Plum sago
- Potatoes jacket
- Potatoes soufflé
- Potatoes au gratin
- Prune whip
- Queen pudding
- Rabbit stewed
- Rice boiled
- Rice water
- Sauce cream roux
- Sauce cream blended
- Sago cream
- Scones
- Siberian cream
- Soup cream
- Soup cream of carrot
- Soup asparagus
- Soup chicken
- Soup celery
- Soup onion
- Soup oyster
- Soup fish
- Soup tomato
- Soup potato
- Sponge cakes
- Stewed fruit
- Sweetbreads in sauce
- Sweetbreads fried
- Sweet white sauce
- Tea
- Tea punch
- Toast
- Toast water
- Tomato juice
- Trifle
- Tripe stewed
- Veal broth
- Whiting au gratin
- Wine jelly
- Wine whey

195-?

The Army and Navy Recipe Book. (Army and Navy Stores, 195-?) [Hoyle 45]
Recipes (pp37-38)
- Beef tea
- Chicken or veal panada
- Stewed pigeon
- Raw beef sandwiches
- A cup of arrowroot
- Tapioca pudding

1950

More About Cooking. (Oakley, 1950) [Hoyle 1006]
Recipe (p11)
- Bran tea

ALPHABETICAL TITLE LIST

Short Title	Reference
192 of the Best Recipes for Rice.	(Rice Marketing Board of New South Wales, 1933)
400 Tested Recipes.	(McCall & McCall, 1903)
600 Tested Recipes.	(Auburn Methodist Church, 1906)
A Friend in the Kitchen.	(Colcord, 1898)
A Handbook of Home Management.	(The Department of Education Victoria, 194-?)
A Small Collection of Plain Cookery Recipes.	(Bishop, 1911)
Adelaide Cookery Note Book for Domestic Economy Pupils.	(Hills, 1902)
Adelect Invalid and Convalescent Cookery.	(Benson, 1942)
Advanced Hygiene How to cure disease without recourse to drugs or medicine of any kind.	(Hern, 1892)
Albion Park Scotch Fair Cookery Book.	(Miller, 1909)
"All in One" Recipe Book and Household Guide.	(Cox, 1925)
An Outline of Cookery.	(Red Cross Emergency Service, 194-?)
Armidale Red Cross Cookery Book.	(Armidale Branch Red Cross Society, 1920)
Army and Navy Recipe Book.	(Army and Navy Stores, 195-?)
Art of Living in Australia.	(Muskett, 1893)
Attainment of Health and the Treatment of the Different Diseases by Means of Diet.	(Muskett, 1908)
Aunt Susan's Recipes.	(Susan, 1920)
Australasian Cookery Book.	(Anon, 1913)
Australia Recipe Book.	(Matheson, 192-?)
Australian Cook: A complete manual of cookery suitable for the Australian colonies.	(Wilkinson, 1877)
Australian Cook and Laundry Book.	(Rawson, 1897)
Australian Cookery Book.	(Eddy, 1935a)
Australian Cookery of Today Illustrated.	(Prudence, 1940)
Australian Cookery Recipes.	(Wicken, 1902)
Australian Economic Cookery Book and Housewife's Companion.	(Story, 1900)
Australian Enquiry Book.	(Rawson, 1895)

Australian Everyday Cookery.	(A Professional Cook, 1913)
Australian Home: A handbook of domestic economy	(Wicken, 1891)
Australian Home Cookery.	(Prudence, 193-?)
Australian Home Cookery.	(Anon, 1914?)
Australian Household Guide.	(Hackett, 1916)
Australian Household Manual.	(Winning, 1898)
Australian Housewife's Guide to Domestic Economy.	(Winning, 1902)
Australian Plain Cookery.	(A Practical Cook, 1882)
Australian Table Dainties.	(Wicken, 1897)
Barker College Cookery Book.	(Turner, 1925)
Barossa Cookery Book.	(Anon, 1917a)
Beefine Way: A range of tested recipes.	(Anon, 1945a)
Bessie Eddy Cookery Book.	(Eddy, 1935b)
Best of Everything Recipe Book.	(The Disabled Mens' Association, 1927)
"Bethany" Cookery Book.	(Bethany Babies Home, 1937)
Blossoms Cookery Book.	(Drummond, 1931)
Book of Diet.	(Muskett, 1898)
Book of Good Housekeeping.	(Good Housekeeping Institute, 1948)
Calling All Cooks!	(Newman, 1940)
Canberra Cookery Book of Good and Tried Recipes.	(Anon, 1927)
"Carry On" Cookery Book.	(King, 1926)
Cassell's Household Cookery.	(Heritage, 1910)
"Central" Cookery Book.	(Irvine, 192-?)
Citrus Recipes for Every Day.	(The Victorian Railways Commissioners in conjuction with The Victorian Central Citrus Association, 1930)
Coles Australian Household Guide; A Universal Domestic Advisor.	(Coles Book Arcade, 1891)
Coles Popular Cookery.	(Payne, 1889)
Colonial Everyday Cookery.	(Anon, 1903)
Colonial Mutual Life Cookery Book.	(Colonial Mutual Life Assurance Society, 1924)
Commonsense Cookery Book.	(The New South Wales Public School Cookery Teachers' Association, 1914)

Common-Sense Hints on Plain Cookery.	(The Cookery Teachers' Association of New South Wales, 1916)
Commonwealth Household, Social and Medical Guide.	(Curtis, 1901)
Cookery: A short course for beginners.	(Education Department of Victoria, 1942)
Cookery Book.	(Beilby, 1935)
Cookery Book.	(Bundaberg Branch of the Country Women's Association, 1931)
Cookery Book.	(Fletcher Chester & Co, 1926)
Cookery Book.	(Voss, 1934)
Cookery Book Mainly for Nurses and Bachelor Girls.	(Shepherd, 192-?)
Cookery Book: Over 500 tested recipes.	(Country Women's Association Queensland - Nambour Branch, 1944)
Cookery Book: Tried and tested recipes.	(The Women's Guild of St Peter's Church of England Croydon, 192-?)
Cookery Class Recipes: As taught in the kitchens of the Metropolitan Gas Company.	(Ross, 1900)
Cooking Craft.	(Nash, 1926)
Cookery for Common Ailments.	(A Fellow of the Royal College of Physicians & Browne, 1911)
Cookery for Invalids, Convalescents and Children.	(Kirkhope, 1940, 1944)
Cookery for Invalids.	(Schauer & Schauer, 1912)
Cookery Instruction Card (set of 33 cards).	(Victoria Department of Public Instruction, 191-?)
Cookery Recipes for the People.	(Pearson, 1889)
Cook's Guide and Housekeeper's and Butler's Assistant.	(Francatelli, 1884)
Coronation Cookery Book.	(Sawyer & Moore-Sims, 1936)
Coronation Cookery Book.	(Wilson, 1911)
Cottage Cookery by "Rita".	(Vaile, 1897)
Course of Four Lectures on Sick Nursing.	(Hamilton, 1886)
CWA Cookery Book and Household Hints.	(Barnes, 1941)
Dainty Dishes.	(Nestlé, 194-?)
Dainty Dishes: A book of selected recipes by Nestle's.	(Nestlé, 192-?)
Dainty Dishes for Children, Invalids and Convalescents.	(Drake & Giles, Between 1923 and 1929)
Davis Dainty Dishes.	(Davis Gelatine (Australia), 1924)
Delicious Milk Dishes and Drinks.	(Milk Board Melbourne, 1936)

Diet Lists for Australian Medical Practitioners.	(Springthorpe & Mullins, 1896)
Diets: Eating for health.	(Flay, 1938)
Domestic Science Handbook (NSW).	(New South Wales Cookery Teachers Association, 1937)
Domestic Science Handbook (Vic).	(Department of Education Victoria, 1938)
Dr Chase's Third Last and Complete Receipt Book and Household Physician.	(Chase, 1887)
Dr Holbrook's American Cookery.	(Holbrook, 1888)
Economic Cookery and Invalid Dishes.	(Bile Bean, 1903)
Economic Housewife's Guide to Cookery.	(May, 1894)
Electric Cookery Book.	(State Electricity Commission of Victoria, 193-?)[
Electric Refrigerator Recipes and Menus.	(Bradley & others, 1927)
Elementary Cookery Book.	(Miller & Miller, 1903)
Elementary Text Book of Cookery, Laundry and Home Management.	(The New South Wales Public School Cookery Teachers' Association, 1946)
English and Australian Cookery Book.	(Abbott, 1864)
Every Woman's Domestic Companion.	(Anon, 1912)
"Everylady's" Cook Book containing over 600 recipes.	(White, 1915)
Everylady's Cook-Book.	(Drake, 1924)
Everything a Lady Should Know.	(Anon, 1914)
Excell Cook Book.	(Aronson, 1923)
For Invalids and Convalescents.	(Davis Gelatine Cookery Department, Between 1938 and 1940)
Glennen's Cook Book.	(Glennen, 1913)
Golden Cookery Book.	(Anon, 194-?-a)
Golden Recipes.	(W White and Co, 19-?)
Golden Wattle Cookery Book.	(Wylie, 1924)
Good Health Cookery Book.	(Kress, 1907)
Good Health: Cookery book and food manual.	(Harris, 1939)
Goulburn Cookery Book.	(Rutledge, 1899)
Green and Gold Cookery Book.	(Anon, 1925)
Guild Cookery Book.	(Ladies Working Guild, 1909)
Hamilton Cookery Book of Tried Recipes.	(Simpson & Gummov, 1915)
Healthful Cookery.	(Bartlett, 1932)

Hobart Cookery Book of Tested Recipes, Household Hints and Home Remedies.	(Committee of Ladies for the Methodist Central Mission Melville Street Hobart, 1908)
Home and Health: A household manual.	(A Competent Committee of Home-makers and Physicians, 1909)
Home Cookery and Jewish Recipes.	(Marks, 192-?)
Home Cookery for Australia: All tested recipes.	(Presbyterian Women's Missionary Union of Victoria, 1904)
Home Golden Cookery Book.	(Anon, 193-?-a)
Home Nursing: Feeding the convalescent.	(Dateba, 1925)
Homecraft Book: A work compiled for the home lover.	(Victorian Association of Creches, 1941)
Household Book.	(Victorian Children's Aid Society Home, 1940)
Householder's Friend.	(Naylor, 192-?)
Housekeeping for Two or More.	(Winning, 1915)
Housewife's Shopping Guide and Cookery Book.	(The Progressive Publicity Company, 1924)
Invalid and Convalescent Cookery.	(Harriott, 1912)
Invalid and Convalescent Cookery for Hospital Trainees.	(Butler, Between 1930 and 1935)
Invalid Cookery.	(Queensland Department of Public Instruction, 1929)
Invalid Cookery: A text book for hospital trainees.	(Missingham, 1949)
Invalid Cookery: Recipes used in nurses' cookery classes and approved by the ATNA.	(Fowler, 1922)
Invalid Cookery Class Recipes: As taught in the kitchen of the Metropolitan Gas Company Melbourne.	(Ross, 1917)
It's in Your Kitchen.	(Parry, 1936)
J.G. Hanks & Co's Cookery Guide.	(Wicken, 1890b)
J.H. Redmond Cookery Book and Household Guide.	(Redmond, 1912)
Keeyunga Cookery Book.	(McGowan, 1911)
Kindergarten Cookery Book.	(Kindergarten Union of New South Wales, 1924)
Kingswood Cookery Book.	(Wicken, 1888)
Kitchen Front.	(Australian Broadcasting Commission, 1943)
Kookaburra Cookery Book of Culinary and Household	(Committee of the Lady Victoria Buxton Girls' Club, 1911)

Recipes and Hints.	
Kuitpo Cookery Book.	(Anon, 1947)
Ladies Delight Recipe Book.	(Anon, 192-?-a)
Lady Hackett's Household Guide.	(Murphy, 1940)
Leader Spare Corner Book Parts 10, 11, 12: A unique collection of home and household hints & kitchen recipes.	(Anon, Between 1938 and 1940)
Lee's Priceless Recipes.	(Oliver, 1912)
Liberals' Cookery Book.	(Schlank, 1912)
"Lifeguard" Cookery Book.	(Drake, 1922)
Mallee Cookery Book.	(Berri Methodist Ladies Guild, 194-?)
Maltovine Home Guide.	(Maltovine, 1933)
Manual of Domestic Art (Cookery).	(Education Department of South Australia, 1928)
Manual of Home Economics.	(Cullen, 1948)
Marmite.	(Sanitarium Health Food Company, Between 1930 and 1935)
Marmite Recipes.	(Sanitarium Health Food Company, 193-?)
Mary Elizabeth Cook Book.	(Aronson, 1927)
Milk Recipes.	(Milk Board Sydney, 1930?)
Milk Recipes for Young and Old.	(Betterment and Publicity Board Victorian Railways, 1937)
Milky Way Housewife's Book.	(Nestlé, 1916)
Milky Way of Cookery.	(Anon, 194-?-b)
Miss Drake's Home Cookery.	(Drake, 1925)
Miss Fowler's Cook Book	(Fowler, 1910)
Miss Futter's Australian Home Cookery.	(Futter, 1924)
Mission Cookery Book.	(The Mission of St James and St John, 1928)
Modern Advanced Cookery.	(The N.S.W. Cookery Teachers Association, Between 1931 and 1936)
More About Cooking.	(Oakley, 1950)
Mrs. Beeton's All-About Cookery with over 2000 Practical Recipes.	(Beeton, 1923)
Mrs Beeton's Cookery Book.	(Beeton, 1901)
Mrs Carter's Cookery Book.	(Carter, 1926)

Mrs Maclurcan's Cookery Book.	(Maclurcan, 1898)
New Goulburn Cookery Book.	(Rutledge & McCarthy, 1937)
New Idea Cook Book for Australian and New Zealand Housewives.	(White, 1910)
New PWMU Cookery Book.	(Campbell, 1936)
New Zealand Domestic Cookery Book	(Harman & Gard'ner, 1913?)
Notes and Recipes on Invalid Cookery and Nutrition.	(Giles & Rapley, 194-?)
Nursery Cookery Book.	(The Mothercraft Association of Queensland, 1933)
Orange Recipe Gift Book.	(Orange District Hospital Auxiliary, 1931)
Our Cookery Book.	(Pell, 1916)
Our Daily Fare and How to Provide It.	(Anon, 1899a)
Over 100 Ways of Using Bread.	(NSW Bread Industry, 1942)
Pinnaroo Solders' Memorial Cookery Book.	(Anon, 192-?-b)
Pluckings from Medical and Other Works.	(Anon, 19-?)
Popular Co-operative Cookery Book.	(Adelaide Co-operative Stores Limited, 1934)
Practical Australian Cookery.	(Monro, 1912)
Presbyterian Cookery Book of Good and Tried Recipes.	(Women's Missionary Association of the Presbyterian Church of New South Wales, 1962)
Principles of Home Cookery.	(The New South Wales Public School Cookery Teachers' Association, 1926)
Principles of Practical Cookery for School Pupils.	(Rankin, 1905)
Public School Girls' Book of Recipes.	(Teachers of the West Redfern Cookery School, 1908)
PWMU Cookery Book.	(Howat & Miersch, 1973)
PWMU Cookery Book of Victoria.	(The Presbyterian Women's Missionary Union of Victoria, 1921)
Recipe Book.	(The Disabled Mens' Association, 193-?)
Recipes: Secret, selected, practical, original.	(The Wardmaster, 1924)
Recipes for Use in Home Science Classes.	(Blackmore, 194-?)
Recipes Given by Mrs Wicken at Cookery Classes Hobart.	(Wicken, 1890a)
Red Cross Cookery Book: 250 recipes.	(Lowe, 1915)
Red Cross Emergency Cookery Book.	(Newman, 192-?)

Robinson's Cookery Book.	(Naylor, 194-?)
Schauer Cookery Book.	(Schauer & Schauer, 1909)
School of Mines Cookery Book.	(Ross et al., 1930)
Simple Cookery for the People: Easy and economical dishes.	(Senn, 192-?)
Simple Cookery for Use in Itinerant Domestic Schools.	(Queensland Department of Public Instruction, 1924)
Some Tested Recipes.	(Hughes, 1932)
South Australian Presbyterian Cookery Book.	(Chalmers Church Friendship Club, 1924)
Southern Cookery Book.	(Ross et al., 1958)
Southern Cross Domestic Science.	(Anon, 1917b)
St Luke's Cookery Book.	(Higgins, 1932)
St Paul's Cookery Book.	(De Boos, 192-?)
Star Cookery Book.	(The Disabled Mens' Association, 1928)
Stowport Cookery Book of 500 Tested Recipes.	(Burnie Methodist Church Trust, 1930)
Strathalbyn Cookery Book.	(Edgar, 1925)
Swinburne Technical College Glenferrie: Student's text book for home cookery.	(Drake, Between 1915 and 1922)
Sylvia's Cookery Book.	(Farrell, 1914)
Tinned Foods and How to Use Them.	(Anon, 1893)
To Mr and Mrs Newlywed.	(Anon, 1924)
"Truth" and "Daily Mirror" Cookery Book.	(Anon, 1943)
Twentieth Century Cookery Book.	(Anon, 1899b)
Union Jack Cookery Book and Home Companion.	(Union Jack, 1919)
Victorian Country Women's Recipe Book 1945-46.	(Anon, 1945b)
"Victory" Cookery Book.	(Jackson, 1944)
Vitadatio Sick Room Cookery Book and General Recipes.	(Vitadatio, 1899)
War Chest Cookery Book.	(The War Chest Fund, 1917)
Wartime Cookery.	(Dunne, 1945)
"Welfare" Cookery Book.	(Mount Gambier Branch Mothers' and Babies' Health Association, 1930)
What to Eat and When and How and Why.	(Huston, 1913)
Whitcombe's Everyday Cookery for Australia.	(A Professional Cook, 1913)
Windsor Recipe Book.	(Anon, 191-?)

WMU Cookery Book.	(The Queensland Presbyterian Missions, 1908)
Women's Missionary Association of NSW Cookery Book of Good and Tried Receipts.	(MacInnes, 1895)
XXth Century Cooking and Home Decoration.	(Aronson, 1900)
YLG Cookery Book.	(Members of the Young Ladies' Guild, 1916)
Your Own Stores Book of Cookery.	(Eudunda Farmers' Co-operative Society Ltd, 1921)

REFERENCE LIST

A Competent Committee of Home-makers and Physicians. (1909). *Home and Health: A household manual* (2nd ed.). Melbourne: Signs Publishing Company.

A Fellow of the Royal College of Physicians, & Browne, P. (1911). *Cookery for Common Ailments*. Melbourne: Cassell and Company Ltd.

A Practical Cook. (1882). *Australian Plain Cookery* (2nd ed.). Melbourne: AH Massina & Co.

A Professional Cook. (1913). *Australian Everyday Cookery: Hints on carving, preparing menus, laundry work and general housekeeping* (6th ed.). Melbourne: Whitcombe and Tombs Ltd.

Abbott, E. (1864). *The English and Australian Cookbook: Cookery for the many as well as for the 'Upper Ten Thousand' by an Australian aristologist*. London: Sampson, Lowe, Son & Marston.

Adelaide Co-operative Stores Limited. (1934). *The Popular Co-operative Cookery Book*. Adelaide: The Adelaide Co-operative Stores Ltd.

Anon. (19-?). *Pluckings from Medical and Other Works: Handy book of reference for the preservation of health/ also Melbourne Economic Cookery Book.* (8th revised ed.). Melbourne: TM Donaldson & Co.

Anon. (191-?). *The Windsor Recipe Book: Containing 600 recipes*. Melbourne: LA Parks.

Anon. (192-?-a). *The Ladies Delight Recipe Book*. Geelong: SA Joy and Sons (printer).

Anon. (192-?-b). *The Pinnaroo Soldiers' Memorial Cookery Book. Good tried recipes by local ladies.* Pinnaroo: The "Times".

Anon. (192-?-c). *The Tasmanian Home Cookery Book*. Hobart: J Walch & Sons.

Anon. (193-?-a). *The Home Golden Cookery Book*. Bendigo: Boulton Bros (printer).

Anon. (193-?-b). *Whitcombe's Everyday Cookery: 1062 selected and tested recipes, revised by cookery experts and leading dietitians*. Australia, New Zealand, United Kingdom: Whitcombe & Tombs Pty Ltd.

Anon. (194-?-a). *The Golden Cookery Book: With invaluable household recipes, invalid cookery, etc.* Bendigo: Bolton Bros (printer).

Anon. (194-?-b). *The Milky Way of Cookery: 73 Trufood recipes*. Glenormiston, Vic: Trufoods of Australia.

Anon. (1893). *Tinned Foods and How to Use Them*. Melbourne and Sydney: Ward, Lock & Bowden Ltd.

Anon. (1899a). *Our Daily Fare and How To Provide It*. Melbourne: Ward, Lock & Co Ltd.

Anon. (1899b). *The Twentieth Century Cookery Book: Containing choice recipes for household and general use, together with other valuable information*. Brisbane: H Pole & Co.

Anon. (1903). *Colonial Everday Cookery: Containing general rules and practical hints with carefully selected and tested recipes*. Melbourne: Whitcombe & Tombs Ltd.

Anon. (1912). *Every Woman's Domestic Companion: A book of household requirements, over 700 useful recipes including paper bag cookery.* Sydney: George B Philip & Son.

Anon. (1913). *The Australasian Cookery Book. Specially compiled for the requirements of Australian & New Zealand Homes.* Melbourne: Ward, Lock & Co Ltd.

Anon. (1914). *Everything a Lady Should Know: A book of everyday requirements comprising 1100 useful recipes* (12th ed.). Sydney: George B Philip & Son.

Anon. (1914?). *The Australian Home Cookery.* Adelaide: ES Wigg & Sons.

Anon. (1917a). *The Barossa Cookery Book: Issued in conjunction with Tanunda Australia Day September 8 1917* (1st ed.). Tanunda: The Barossa News.

Anon. (1917b). *The Southern Cross Domestic Science: Containing three year courses in cookery, housewifery & laundry work - for schools.* Melbourne: Whitcombe & Tombs Ltd.

Anon. (1924). *To Mr. and Mrs. Newlywed.* Sydney: The leading business firms of Sydney.

Anon. (1925). *Green and Gold Cookery Book* (2nd ed.). Adelaide: Combined Congregational and Baptists Churches of South Australia.

Anon. (1927). *Canberra Cookery Book of Good and Tried Recipes.* Sydney: The NSW Bookstall Co Ltd.

Anon. (1933). *The Barossa Cookery Book: 1000 selected recipes* (3rd ed.). Tanunda: Soldiers' Memorial Institute.

Anon. (1943). *"Truth" and "Daily Mirror" Cookery Book.* Brisbane: "Truth".

Anon. (1945a). *The Beefine Way: A range of tested recipes.* Melbourne: Beefine Pty Ltd.

Anon. (1945b). *The Victorian Country Women's Recipe Book 1945-1946.* Melbourne: Stephen Quick.

Anon. (1947). *The Kuitpo Cookery Book* (6th ed.). Adelaide: Kuitpo Gala Committee.

Anon. (Between 1938 and 1940). *The Leader Spare Corner Book Parts 10, 11, 12: A unique collection of home and household hints & kitchen recipes.* Melbourne: The Age.

Armidale Branch Red Cross Society. (1920). *The Armidale Red Cross Cookery Book of Tested Recipes* (2nd ed.). Armidale: Red Cross Society.

Army and Navy Stores. (195-?). *The Army and Navy Recipe Book.* Adelaide: F Pritchard.

Aronson, Mrs. F. (1900). *XXth Century Cooking and Home Decorating.* Sydney: William Brooks & Co.

Aronson, Mrs. F. (1923). *Excell Cook Book: for the Junior Red Cross, containing 316 selected recipes.* Sydney: Junior Red Cross Society of NSW.

Aronson, Mrs. F. (1927). *The Mary Elizabeth Cook Book: Over 900 recipes (many new) for all homes.* Sydney: George B Philip & Son.

Auburn Methodist Church. (1906). *600 Tested Recipes, compiled by Mrs H Wharton Shaw.* Melbourne: Specator Publishing Company.

Austin, B. R. (1987). *A Bibliography of Australian Cookery Books Published Prior to 1941*. Melbourne: RMIT.

Australian Broadcasting Commission. (1943). *The Kitchen Front*. Sydney: ABC.

Barnes, A. K. (1941). *The CWA Cookery Book and Household Hints* (5th ed.). Perth: The Country Women's Association of Western Australia Inc.

Barnes, A. K. (1986). *The CWA Cookery Book and Household Hints* (38th ed.). Perth and Adelaide: WS Wigg and Song Pty. Ltd.

Bartlett, J. (1932). *Healthful Cookery*. Warburton: Signs Publishing Co.

Beeton, I. M. (192-?). *Mrs Beeton's Cookery Book: All about cookery, househould work, marketing, trussing carving etc* (Coles Special Edition ed.). Melbourne: EW Cole.

Beeton, I. M. (1901). *Mrs Beeton's Cookery Book: A household guide, all about cookery, household work, marketing, prices, provisions, trussing, serving, carving, menus, etc. etc*. Hobart: J Walch.

Beeton, I. M. (1923). *Mrs. Beeton's All-About Cookery with over 2000 Practical Recipes* (New ed.). Melbourne: Ward, Lock & Co Ltd.

Beeton, I. M. (1928). *Mrs. Beeton's Everyday Cookery with about 2,500 Practical Recipes*. Melbourne: Ward, Locke & Co Ltd.

Beeton, I. M. (1950). *Mrs. Beeton's Family cookery with nearly 3,000 Practical Recipes* (2nd ed.). Melbourne: Ward, Lock & Co Ltd.

Beilby, S. (1935). *Cookery Book*. Adelaide: Federal Printing House.

Benson, G. (1942). *Adelect Invalid and Convalescent Cookery*. Adelaide: The Adelaide Electric Supply Company Ltd.

Berri Methodist Ladies Guild. (194-?). *The Mallee Cookery Book*. Adelaide: Hunkin, Ellis & King (printer).

Bethany Babies Home. (1937). *"Bethany" Cookery Book. 700 tested recipes*. Geelong: Bethany Babies Home.

Betterment and Publicity Board Victorian Railways. (1937). *Milk recipes for Young and Old*. Melbourne: Victorian Railways.

Bile Bean. (1903). *Economic Cookery and Invalid Dishes*. Sydney: Bile Bean Manufacturing Co. Turner and Henderson (printer).

Bishop, A. (1911). *A Small Collection of Plain Cookery Recipes: For household use*. Adelaide: JH Sherring & Co.

Blackmore, M. (194-?). *Recipes for Use in Home Science Classes* (9th ed.). Melbourne, Sydney, Perth: Whitcombe & Tombs Ltd.

Bradley, A., & others. (1927). *Electric Refrigerator Recipes and Menus*. Sydney: Australian General Electric Refrigerator Co. Ltd.

Bundaberg Branch of the Country Women's Association. (1931). *Bundaberg Branch Cookery Book* (2nd ed.). Brisbane: Watson, Ferguson & Co. Ltd.

Burnie Methodist Church Trust. (1930). *Stowport Cookery Book of 500 Tested Recipes*. Burnie: "The Advocate" (printer).

Butler, E. E. (Between 1930 and 1935). *Invalid and Convalescent Cookery for Hospital Trainees. A text book containing lecture notes and recipes required by the ATNA*. Perth: Brokensha & Shaw Ltd.

Campbell, A. (1936). *The New PWMU Cookery Book* (Third impression ed.). Melbourne: The Presbyterian Women's Missionary Union of Victoria.

Carter, A. (1926). *Mrs. Carter's Cookery Book*. Tamworth: John Hammill and Son (printer).

Chalmers Church Friendship Club. (1924). *South Australian Presbyterian Cookery Book*. Adelaide: Gillingham Swan & Co Ltd.

Chase, A. W. (1887). *Dr Chase's Third Last and Complete Receipt Book and Household Physician*. Sydney: Malcolm & Grigg.

Colcord, A. L. (1898). *A Friend in the Kitchen or What to Cook and How to Cook It* (1st ed.). Melbourne: Echo Publishing Co Ltd.

Coles Book Arcade. (1891). *Coles Australian Household Guide; A Universal Domestic Advisor: Comprising the new and enlarged edition of Mrs. Beeton's cookery book*. Melbourne: EW Cole.

Colonial Mutual Life Assurance Society. (1924). *The Colonial Mutual Life Cookery Book*. Melbourne: Colonial Mutual Life Assurance Society Ltd.

Committee of Ladies for the Methodist Central Mission Melville Street Hobart. (1908). *Hobart Cookery Book of Tested Recipes, Household Hints and Home Remedies*. Hobart: Davies Brothers Ltd.

Committee of the Lady Victoria Buxton Girls' Club. (1911). *The Kookaburra Cookery Book of Culinary and Household Recipes and Hints*. Adelaide: Pearsons' Printing House.

Committee of the Lady Victoria Buxton Girls' Club. (1915). *The Kookaburra Cookery Book of Culinary and Household Recipes and Hints* (2nd ed.). Melbourne: E.W Cole.

Country Women's Association Queensland - Nambour Branch. (1944). *Cookery Book: Over 500 tested recipes* (4th ed.). Nambour: McFadden & Sons.

Cox, M. G. V. (1925). *The "All in One" Recipe Book and Household Guide*. Melbourne: Disabled Men's Association of Australia.

Cullen, F. M. (1948). *Manual of Home Economics: In 4 sections comprising cookery theory, food study, laundry work and home management*. Sydney and Brisbane: William Brooks & Co. Ltd.

Curtis, T. (Ed.) (1901). *The Commonwealth Household, Social and Medical Guide*. Sydney: JW Eeedy (printer).

Dateba. (1925). Home Nursing: Feeding the convalescent. *The Australian Woman's Mirror, 1*(32 [30 June]), 21.

Davis Gelatine (Australia). (1924). *Davis Dainty Dishes* (3rd ed.). Sydney: Davis Gelatine (Australia) Ltd.

Davis Gelatine (Australia). (1937). *Davis Dainty Dishes* (Revised ed.). Sydney: Davis Gelatine (Australia) Pty Ltd.

Davis Gelatine Cookery Department. (Between 1938 and 1940). *For Invalids and Convalescents*. Sydney: Davis Gelatine (Australia) Pty Ltd.

Davis Gelatine Department of Home Economics. (196-?). *Ulcer Diets & Recipes for Convalescents*. Botany: Davis Gelatine (Australia) Pty Ltd.

De Boos, P. (192-?). *St Paul's Cookery Book*. Euroa: Gazette Printing and Publishing House.

Department of Education Victoria. (1938). *Domestic Science Handbook: Issued to pupils of girls' schools and domestic art centres*. Melbourne: Osboldstone & Co Pty Ltd.

Department of Education Victoria. (1940). *Domestic Science Handbook for use by the pupils of domestic science school* (6th ed.). Melbourne: Osboldstone & Co Pty Ltd.

Drake, L. (1922). *The "Lifeguard" Cookery Book*. Melbourne: Robertson & Mullens Ltd.

Drake, L. (1924). *Everylady's Cook-Book* (1st ed.). Melbourne: Fitchett Brothers Pty Ltd.

Drake, L. (1925). *Miss Drake's Home Cookery* (6th ed.). Melbourne: Keating-Wood Press.

Drake, L. (Between 1915 and 1922). *Swinburne Technical College Glenferrie: Students' text book for home cookery*. Melbourne: M Hearne and Co.

Drake, L., & Giles, D. M. (1939). *Dainty Dishes for Children, Invalids and Convalescents* (4th ed.). Melbourne: JR Drake.

Drake, L., & Giles, D. M. (Between 1923 and 1929). *Dainty Dishes for Children, Invalids and Convalescents: Swinburne Technical College textbook for Nurses' Cookery Certificate required by the Royal Victorian Trained Nurses' Association*. Box Hill: Reporter Print.

Drummond, A. (1931). *The Blossoms Cookery Book*. Adelaide: Hunkin, Ellis & King Ltd.

Dunne, S. (1945). *Wartime Cookery*. Caulfield, Vic: Edgar H Baillie.

Eddy, B. (1935a). *Australian Cookery Book*. Melbourne: Exchange Press Pty Ltd.

Eddy, B. (1935b). *Bessie Eddy Cookery Book*. South Melbourne: JL Anderson and Sons.

Edgar, A. (1925). *Strathalbyn Cookery Book No 2*. Gin Gin, WA: Braille and Advancement Society for the Blind of Western Australia.

Education Department of South Australia. (1928). *Manual of Domestic Art (Cookery)*. Adelaide: The Education Department.

Education Department of Victoria. (1942). *Cookery: A short course for beginners*. Melbourne: WM Houston, Government Printer.

Eudunda Farmers' Co-operative Society Ltd. (1921). *Your Own Stores Book of Cookery*. Adelaide: O. Ziegler.

Farrell, K. (1914). *Sylvia's Cookery Book*. Launceston: Launceston Examiner.

Flay, S. (1938). *Diets: Eating for health*. Caulfield, Vic: Edgar H Bailie for United Press.

Fletcher Chester & Co. (1926). *Cookery Book*. Melbourne: The Federated Press.

Fowler, L. F. (1910). *Miss Fowler's Cook Book*. Melbourne: George Robertson & Co Pty Ltd.

Fowler, L. F. (1922). *Invalid Cookery: Recipes used in nurses' cookery classes and approved by the ATNA*. Adelaide: G Wood Son & Co.

Francatelli, C. E. (1884). *The Cook's guide and Housekeeper's and Butler's Assistant. A practical treatise on English and foreign cookery in all its branches*. Melbourne: George Robertson & Co Ltd.

Futter, E. (1924). *Australian Home Cookery* (2nd ed.). Sydney: George B Philip & Son.

Giles, D. M., & Rapley, E. M. (194-?). *Notes and Recipes on Invalid Cookery and Nutrition*. Melbourne: Emily McPherson College.

Glennen, M. (1913). *Glennen's Cook Book: Written specially for those interested in preparing food for invalids, diabetics and infants* (2nd ed.). Brisbane: Gordon & Gotch.

Good Housekeeping Institute. (1948). *The Book of Good Housekeeping* (First Australian ed.). Sydney: The National Magazine Company Pty Ltd.

Hackett, D. (1916). *The Australian Household Guide*. Perth: ES Wigg & Son Ltd.

Hamilton, M. (1886). *A Course of Four Lectures delivered to the Members of the Clunes Girls' Friendly Society on Sick Nursing*. Clunes: Guardian and Gazette.

Harman, R., & Gard'ner, S. (1913?). *The New Zealand Domestic Cookery Book* (5th ed.). Melbourne: Whitcombe & Tombs Ltd.

Harriott, K. (1912). *Invalid and Convalescent Cookery. A collection of tried recipes for the use of Australian nurses* (1st ed.). Sydney: NSW Bookstall Co. Ltd.

Harriott, K. (1922). *Invalid and Convalescent Cookery. A collection of tried recipes for the use of Australian nurses* (2nd ed.). Sydney: Williams Brooks & Co Ltd.

Harris, G. (Ed.) (1939). *Good Health: Cookery book and food manual* (1st ed.). Adelaide: The Housewives' Association (SA Div).

Heritage, L. (1910). *Cassell's Household Cookery*. Melbourne: EW Cole.

Hern, J. (1892). *Advanced Hygiene: How to cure disease without recourse to drugs or medicines of any kind*. Melbourne: EW Cole.

Higgins, D. I. (1932). *St. Luke's Cookery Book* (1st ed.). Darlinghurst: Marchant & Co (printer).

Hills, A. (1902). *The Adelaide Cookery Note Book for Domestic Economy Pupils*. Adelaide: The Education Department.

Holbrook, M. (1888). *Dr Holbrook's American Cookery: With an Australian appendix of over 100 refreshing drinks for all seasons*. Melbourne: EW Cole.

Home Economics Institute of Australia (NSW Division). (2013). *The Commonsense Cookery Book* (Centenary ed.). Sydney: Angus & Robertson.

Howat, V., & Miersch, G. (Eds.). (1973). *PWMU Cookery Book* (Revised metric ed.). Melbourne: Lothian Publishing Co.

Hoyle, J. (2010). *An Annotated Bibliography of Australian Domestic Cookery Books 1860s to 1950*. Willoughby NSW: Billycan Cook.

Hughes, G. (1932). *Some Tested Recipes*. Melbourne: The Colonial Gas Association Ltd.

Huston, J. (1913). *What to Eat and When and How and Why: What to do by natural methods to recover health and prevent disease*. Adelaide: The Emmanuel Society.

Irvine, A. (192-?). *"Central" Cookery Book*. Hobart: HT Whiting Pty Ltd.

Irvine, A. (Between 1935 and 1939). *"Central" Cookery Book* (3rd ed.). Hobart: HT Whiting Pty Ltd.

Irwin, A., & Fox, D. (1940). *The Better Housekeeping Bureau Cook Book*. Melbourne: The Better Housekeeping Bureau.

Jackson, L. (1944). *The "Victory" Cookery Book*. Melbourne: J Roy Stevens (printer).

Kindergarten Union of New South Wales. (1924). *The Kindergarten Cookery Book* (2nd ed.). Sydney: The Kindergarten Union.

King, A. J. (1926). *"Carry On" Cookery Book* (5th ed.). Lismore: The Northern Star.

Kirkhope, M. G. (1940). *Cookery for Invalids, Convalescents and Children* (1st ed.). Melbourne: Robertson & Mullens Ltd.

Kirkhope, M. G. (1944). *Cookery for Invalids, Convalescents and Children* (2nd ed.). Melbourne: Robertson & Mullens Ltd.

Kress, L. (1907). *Good Health Cookery Book*. Wharburton: Signs Publishing Company.

Ladies Working Guild. (1909). *Guild Cookery Book*. Port Melbourne: Holy Trinity Church Port Melbourne.

Lowe, N. (1915). *The Red Cross Cookery Book: 250 recipes*. Sydney: Carter's Printing Works.

MacInnes, M. (Ed.) (1895). *Women's Missionary Association Cookery Book of Good and Tried Receipts* (3rd ed.). Sydney: ST Leigh & Co.

Maclurcan, H. (1898). *Mrs. Maclurcan's Cookery Book. A collection of practical recipes specially suitable for Australia* (2nd ed.). Townsville: T Willmett & Sons.

Maltovine. (1933). *The Maltovine Home Guide*. Sydney: The Proprietors of Maltovine.

Marks, H. (192-?). *Home Cookery and Jewish Recipes*. St Kilda, Vic: Wallman & Co (printer).

Matheson, W. (192-?). *The Australia Recipe Book*. Geelong: SA Joy & Sons (printer).

May, M. W. (1894). *The Economic Housewife's and Beekeeper's Guide to Cookery*. West Maitland: E Tipper (printer).

McCall, K., & McCall, Q. (1903). *400 Tested Recipes*. Melbourne: Arbuckle, Waddell & Fawkner.

McGowan, H. C. (1911). *The Keeyunga Cookery Book*. Melbourne: Thomas C Lothian.

Members of the Young Ladies' Guild. (1916). *The YLG Cookery Book*. Launceston: The Young Ladies' Guild, Westbury Tasmania.

Milk Board Melbourne. (1936). *Delicious Milk Dishes and Drinks*. Melbourne: Victorian Milk Producers and Retail Dairymen's Association.

Milk Board Sydney. (1930?). *Milk Recipes*. Sydney: Milk Board.

Miller, E. B., & Miller, J. A. (1903). *Elementary Cookery Book*. Christchurch and Melbourne: Whitcombe & Tombs Ltd.

Miller, M. (1909). *The Albion Park Scotch Fair Cookery Book*. Sydney: The Worker Trade Union Print.

Minot, G., & Murphy, W. (1926). Treatment of pernicious anaemia by a special diet. *Journal of the American Medical Association, 87*, 470-476.

Missingham, F. (1949). *Invalid Cookery: A text book for hospital trainees*. Perth: Technical College Perth.

Monro, A. M. (1912). *The Practical Australian Cookery: A collection of up-to-date tried recipes for domestic and general use* (3rd - revised and enlarged ed.). Sydney: Dymock's Book Arcade.

Mount Gambier Branch Mothers' and Babies' Health Association. (1930). *"Welfare" Cookery Book*. Mount Gambier: Mount Gambier Branch Mothers' and Babies' Health Association,.

Murphy, D. B. M. (1940). *Lady Hackett's Household Guide*. Melbourne: Robertson & Mullens Ltd.

Muskett, P. (1898). *The Book of Diet: With, also, a collection of savoury, choice, delicious, and selected recipes*. Mebourne: George Robertson & Co.

Muskett, P. (1908). *The Attainment of Health; and the Treatment of Different Diseases by Means of Diet*. Sydney: William Brooks & Co Ltd.

Muskett, P. E. (1893). *The Art of Living in Australia*. Melbourne: Eyre and Spottiswoode.

Nash, S. E. (1926). *Cooking Craft*. Melbourne: Sir Isaac Pitman & Sons Ltd.

Naylor, W. (192-?). *The Householder's Friend*. Malvern: Reaby & Co (printer).

Naylor, W. (194-?). *Robinson's Cookery Book*. Malvern: Reaby & Co (printer).

Nestlé. (192-?). *Dainty Dishes: A book of selected recipes by Nestlé's*. Sydney: Nestlé and Anglo-Swiss Condensed Milk Company (Australasia) Ltd.

Nestlé. (194-?). *Dainty Dishes: A book of selected recipes by Nestlé*. Sydney: Nestlé Co Ltd.

Nestlé. (1916). *The Milky Way Housewife's Book: Containing one hundred recipes for making puddings, blancmanges, ices, etc with Nestlé's milk*. Sydney: Nestlé & Anglo-Swiss Condensed Milk Co.

New South Wales Cookery Teachers Association. (1937). *Domestic Science Handbook. For use by pupils of domestic science schools* (3rd ed.). Sydney: New South Wales Cookery Teachers Association,.

Newman, L. (192-?). *Red Cross Emergency Service Cookery Book: Cookery course for volunteer service detachments.* Adelaide: Red Cross Emergency Service Committee.

Newman, L. (1940). *Calling All Cooks!* (1st ed.). Adelaide: South Australian Gas Company.

NSW Bread Industry. (1942). *Over 100 Ways of Using Bread: Tasty and delightful dishes.* Sydney: Cumberland Newspapers Ltd.

Oakley, E. B. I. (1950). *More About Cooking.* Melbourne: [No publishing or printing information].

Oliver, N. (1912). *Lee's Priceless Recipes: The standard collection of famous formulas and simple methods* (Thoroughly Revised ed.). Sydney: The Australian News Company Ltd.

Orange District Hospital Auxiliary. (1931). *The Orange Recipe Gift Book* (3rd ed.). Orange: The Leader Office.

Parry, A. B. (1936). *It's In Your Kitchen: Simple remedies and hints for everyone.* Sydney: Angus & Robertson Ltd.

Payne, A. (1889). *Cole's Popular Cookery.* Melbourne: EW Cole.

Payne, A. (1898). *Cassell's Shilling Cookery.* London, Melbourne: Cassell and Company Ltd.

Pearson, M. (1894). *Cookery Recipes for the People* (3rd ed.). Melbourne: H Hearne & Co.

Pearson, M. J. (1889). *Cookery Recipes for the People.* Melbourne: The Australasian-American Trading Company Ltd.

Pell, F. (1916). *Our Cookery Book* (1st ed.). Melbourne: George Robertson & Co Pty Ltd.

Presbyterian Women's Missionary Union of Victoria. (1904). *Home Cookery for Australia: All tested recipes* (1st ed.). Melbourne: Gordon & Gotch.

Presbyterian Women's Missionary Union of Victoria. (1906). *Home Cookery for Australia: All tested recipes* (2nd ed.). Melbourne: Gordon & Gotch.

Prudence. (193-?). *Australian Home Cookery. 850 tested recipes and practical hints on marketing, invalid cookery, preserves, pickles, beverages, parties, carving, table arrangement, preparing menus and culinary terms.* Melbourne: Ideal Home Library.

Prudence. (1940). *Australian Cookery of Today Illustrated.* Melbourne: The Sun News-Pictorial.

Queensland Department of Public Instruction. (1924). *Simple Cookery for Use in Itinerant Domestic Schools.* Brisbane: Anthony James Cumming Government Printer.

Queensland Department of Public Instruction. (1929). *Invalid Cookery.* Brisbane: Queensland Government.

Rankin, H. (1905). *Principles of Practical Cookery for School Pupils.* Sydney: William Brooks & Co.

Rawson, L. (1895). *The Australian Enquiry Book* (2nd ed.). Melbourne: Pater & Knapton.

Rawson, L. (1897). *Australian Cook and Laundry Book*. Melbourne: KW Knapton & Co.

Red Cross Emergency Service. (194-?). *An Outline of Cookery*. Melbourne: Australian Red Cross Society.

Redmond, J. (1912). *The J.H. Redmond Cookery Book and Household Guide*. Melbourne: JH Redmond.

Rice Marketing Board of New South Wales. (1933). *192 of the Best Recipes for Rice: The food of the people*. Leeton: Rice Marketing Board for the State of NSW.

Ross, B. E., Batchelor, M. G., Kinnear, E. W., & Crossley, H. S. (1930). *School of Mines Cookery Book* (1st ed.). Adelaide: The Advertiser Office.

Ross, B. E., Batchelor, M. G., Kinnear, E. W., & Crossley, H. S. (1936). *School of Mines Cookery Book* (2nd ed.). Adelaide: The Advertiser.

Ross, B. E., Batchelor, M. G., Kinnear, E. W., & Crossley, H. S. (1944). *School of Mines Cookery Book* (3rd ed.). Adelaide: The Advertiser.

Ross, B. E., Batchelor, M. G., Kinnear, E. W., & Crossley, H. S. (1958). *The Southern Cookery Book (Formerly known as the School of Mines Cookery Book)* (5th ed.). Adelaide: Rigby Ltd.

Ross, I. (1900). *Cookery Class Recipes: As taught in the kitchens of the Metropolitan Gas Company, Melbourne*. Melbourne: Echo Publishing Company Ltd.

Ross, I. (1917). *Invalid Cookery Class Recipes: As taught in the kitchen of the Metropolitan Gas Company, Melbourne* (3rd (?) ed.). Melbourne: Anderson, Gowan & Du Rieu Ptd Ltd (printer).

Rutledge, J. (1899). *The Goulburn Cookery Book* (Facsimile edition 1975 from The National Trust ed.). Sydney: Hogbin, Poole Pty Ltd (printer).

Rutledge, J. (1913). *The Goulburn Cookery Book* (13th ed.). Sydney: Edwards, Dunlop & Co. Ltd.

Rutledge, M. F., & McCarthy, W. (1937). *The New Goulburn Cookery Book* (39th ed.). Sydney: WE Smith Ltd.

Sanitarium Health Food Company. (193-?). *Marmite Recipes: Marmite cookery book*. Sydney: Sanitarium Health Food Company.

Sanitarium Health Food Company. (Between 1930 and 1935). *Marmite*. Sydney: Sanitarium Health Food Company.

Sawyer, J., & Moore-Sims, S. (1936). *The Coronation Cookery Book: Compiled for the Country Women's Association of NSW* (1st ed.). Sydney: Publicity Press.

Schauer, A. (1918). *The Schauer Cookery Book: With which is incorporated The Invalid Cookery Book* (4th ed.). Brisbane: WR Smith & Paterson.

Schauer, A., & Leese, M. (1946). *The Schauer Australian Cookery Book* (9th ed.). Brisbane: WR Smith & Paterson Pty. Ltd.

Schauer, A., & Schauer, M. (1909). *The Schauer Cookery Book* (1st ed.). Brisbane: Edwards Dunlop & Co.

Schauer, A., & Schauer, M. (1912). *Cookery for Invalids: For hospital and home, nurses in training schools, in private practice, and others who tend the sick* (2nd ed.). Brisbane: Edwards, Dunlop & Co Ltd.

Schlank, R. (1912). *The Liberals' Cookery Book: Being good and tried recipes contributed by ladies from all parts of South Australia.* Adelaide: Adelaide Women's Branch of the Liberals' Union.

Senn, C. H. (192-?). *Simple Cookery for the People: Easy and economical dishes.* Melbourne: Ward, Lock & Co Ltd.

Shepherd, M. (192-?). *Cookery Book Mainly for Nurses and Bachelor Girls* (4th ed.). Sydney: MP Shepherd?

Simpson, A., & Gummov, F. (1915). *The Hamilton Cookery Book of Tried Recipes* (2nd ed.). Hamilton, Vic: Osborn Mannett (printer).

Springthorpe, J., & Mullins, G. L. (1896). *Diet Lists for Australian Medical Practitioners.* Sydney: Angus & Robertson.

State Electricity Commission of Victoria. (193-?). *Electric Cookery Book.* Melbourne: State Electricity Commission of Victoria.

Story, F. F. (1900). *Australian Economic Cookery Book and Housewife's Companion* (2nd ed.). Sydney: Kealy & Philip.

Susan, A. (1920). *Aunt Susan's Recipes: A collection of tried and palatable dishes - simple and economical.* Adelaide: Vardon & Sons Ltd.

Teachers of the West Redfern Cookery School. (1908). *The Public School Girls' Book of Recipes.* Sydney and Brisbane: William Brooks & Co Ltd.

The Cookery Teachers' Association of New South Wales. (1916). *Common-Sense Hints on Plain Cookery: A companion volume to the Common-Sense Cookery Book, explaining all methods of preparing food.* Sydney: Angus & Robertson.

The Department of Education Victoria. (194-?). *A Handbook of Home Management: Issued to the pupils of girls' schools and domestic art centres.* Melbourne: Osboldstone & Co Pty Ltd.

The Disabled Mens' Association. (193-?). *Recipe Book: Containing all the best culinary recipes, formulas and menus.* Melbourne: The Disabled Men's Association of Australia.

The Disabled Mens' Association. (1927). *The Best of Everything Recipe Book.* Melbourne: DMA Pty Ltd.

The Disabled Mens' Association. (1928). *The Star Recipe Book.* Adelaide: DMA Pty Ltd.

The Mission of St James and St John. (1928). *The Mission Cookery Book.* Melbourne: Farrow Falcon Press.

The Mothercraft Association of Queensland. (1933). *The Nursery Cookery Book.* Brisbane: Jackson & Sullivan (printer).

The N.S.W. Cookery Teachers Association. (1931). *The Commonsense Cookery Book* (New and enlarged ed.). Sydney: Angus & Robertson.

The N.S.W. Cookery Teachers Association. (Between 1931 and 1936). *Modern Advanced Cookery*. Sydney: George B Philip & Son.

The N.S.W. Public School Cookery Teachers' Association. (1948). *The Advanced Commonsense Cookery Book*. Sydney: Angus and Robertson.

The N.S.W. Public School Cookery Teachers' Association. (1974). *The Commonsense Cookery Book* (Metric ed.). Sydney: Angus & Robertson.

The New South Wales Public School Cookery Teachers' Association. (1914). *The Commonsense Cookery Book* (1st ed.). Sydney: Angus & Robertson.

The New South Wales Public School Cookery Teachers' Association. (1926). *Principles of Home Cookery*. Sydney: The New South Wales Public School Cookery Teachers' Association.

The New South Wales Public School Cookery Teachers' Association. (1946). *Elementary Text Book of Cookery, Laundry and Home Management*. Sydney: The New South Wales Cookery Teachers' Association.

The New South Wales Public School Cookery Teachers' Association. (1970). *The Commonsense Cookery Book* (Revised ed.). Sydney: Angus and Roberston.

The Presbyterian Women's Missionary Union of Victoria. (1921). *PWMU Cookery Book of Victoria* (4th ed.). Melbourne: Brown, Prior & Co Ltd.

The Progressive Publicity Company. (1924). *The Housewife's Shopping Guide and Cookery Book*. Perth: EB Bayliss.

The Queensland Presbyterian Missions. (1908). *WMU Cookery Book of over 588 Tried Recipes: In aid of the Queensland Presbyterian Missions* (7th ed.). Brisbane: WR Smith & Paterson.

The Victorian Railways Commissioner for the Federal Citrus Council of Australia. (1948). *Citrus Recipes for Every Day*. Melbourne: Victorian Railways.

The Victorian Railways Commissioners in conjuction with The Victorian Central Citrus Association. (1930). *Citrus Recipes for Every Day*. Melbourne: Victorian Railways.

The War Chest Fund. (1917). *The War Chest Cookery Book*. Sydney: Websdale, Shoosmith Ltd (printer).

The Wardmaster. (1924). *Recipes: Secret, selected, practical, original*. Melbourne: Veritas Publishing Co.

The Women's Guild of St Peter's Church of England Croydon. (192-?). *Cookery Book: Tried and tested recipes*. Sydney: St Peter's Church Croydon. DS Ford (printer).

Trustees of the NSW Cookery Teachers Scholarship Fund. (1988). *The Commonsense Cookery Book*. North Ryde: Angus & Robertson.

Turner, E. (1925). *The Barker College Cookery Book: With hints on first aid, a collection of recipes from mothers and friends of past and present pupils*. Sydney: The Barker College; DS Ford (printer).

Union Jack. (1919). *The Union Jack Cookery Book and Home Companion: The housewives' book of knowledge*. Melbourne: Modern Printing Co. Pty. Ltd.

Vaile, R. (1897). *Cottage Cookery (Hygeienic and Economic) by "Rita"* (2nd ed.). Melbourne: George Robertson & Co.

Victoria Department of Public Instruction. (191-?). *Cookery Instruction Card: Set of 33 cards.* Melbourne: Robert S Brin, Government Printer.

Victorian Association of Creches. (1941). *Homecraft Book: A work compiled for the home lover.* Melbourne: The Victorian Association of Creches.

Victorian Children's Aid Society Home. (1940). *Household Book.* Melbourne: Franklin Press (printer).

Vitadatio. (1899). *Vitadatio Sick Room Cookery Book and General Recipes.* Melbourne: Echo Publishing Co Ltd.

Voss, V. (1934). *Cookery Book* (3rd ed.). Rockhampton: Federal Press Pty Ltd.

W White and Co. (19-?). *Golden Recipes for the Use of All Ages* (8th ed.). Ballarat: EE Campbell.

White, G. S. (1910). *The "New Idea" Cook Book: Containing over 600 recipes tested and proved good.* Melbourne: T Shaw Fitchett.

White, G. S. (1915). *"Everylady's" Cook Book: Containing over 600 recipes tested and proved good* (5th ed.). Melbourne: T Shaw Fitchett.

Wicken, H. F. (1888). *The Kingswood Cookery Book* (2nd ed.). Melbourne: George Robertson & Co.

Wicken, H. F. (1890a). *Recipes Given by Mrs Wicken at the Cookery Class, Hobart: Supplement to Kingswood Cookery Book.* Hobart: Mercury Office.

Wicken, H. F. (1890b). *J.G. Hanks & Co.'s Cookery Guide: The cook's compass.* Sydney: J.G. Hanks and Co.

Wicken, H. F. (1891). *The Australian Home: A Handbook of domestic economy.* Sydney: Edwards Dunlop & Co Ltd.

Wicken, H. F. (1897). *Australian Table Dainties and Appetising Dishes: A handy guide for Australian housekeepers.* Melbourne: Ward, Lock & Co.

Wicken, H. F. (1898). *The Kingswood Cookery Book* (4th ed.). Sydney: Angus & Robertson.

Wicken, H. F. (1902). *Australian Cookery Recipes: A handy guide for Australian housekeepers.* Melbourne: Ward, Lock & Co. Ltd.

Wilkinson, A. J. (1877). *The Australian Cook: A complete manual of cookery suitable for the Australian colonies* (2nd ed.). Melbourne, Sydney, Adelaide: George Robertson.

Wilson, E. (1911). *The Coronation Cookery Book.* Adelaide: WK Thomas & Co (printer).

Winning, Mrs. T. P. (1898). *The Household Manual: A complete household repository of useful information comprising hints on the management of the kitchen, laundry, poultry-yard etc, savoury dishes and invalid diet* (1st ed.). Sydney: Edward Lee & Co (printer).

Winning, Mrs. T. P. (1900). *The Australian Housewife's Guide to Domestic Economy: Comprising hints and advice on home management, economical cookery, invalid diet, domestic remedies, and advice to young mothers* (2nd ed.). Sydney: Kealy & Philip.

Winning, Mrs. T. P. (1915). *Housekeeping for Two or More: Casserole and general cooking* (5th ed.). Melbourne: EW Cole.

Winning, Mrs. T. P. (1902). *The Australian Housewife Guide to Domestic Economy* (2nd ed.). Sydney: Kealy & Philip.

Women's Missionary Association of the Presbyterian Church of New South Wales. (1931). *Cookery Book of Good and Tried Receipts* (20th ed.). Sydney: Angus & Robertson.

Women's Missionary Association of the Presbyterian Church of New South Wales. (1962). *The Presbyterian Cookery Book of Good and Tried Recipes* (New ed.). Sydney: Angus and Robertson.

Wylie, M. A. (1924). *The Golden Wattle Cookery Book* (1st ed.). Perth: ES Wigg & Son.

Wylie, M. A. (1930). *The Golden Wattle Cookery Book* (3rd ed.). Perth: ES Wigg & Son Ltd.

Wylie, M. A. (1931). *The Golden Wattle Cookery Book* (4th ed.). Perth: ES Wigg & Son Ltd.

ABOUT THE AUTHOR

Peter Williams is a Fellow of the Dietitians Association of Australia, an Honorary Professorial Fellow in the School of Medicine at the University of Wollongong and an Adjunct Professor of Nutrition and Dietetics at the University of Canberra.

Before working at the University of Wollongong, Peter was the Director of Scientific and Consumer Affairs at Kellogg (Australia) for three years, and previously was the Chief Dietitian and Food Services Manager at Royal Prince Alfred Hospital in Sydney.

Peter has been an active researcher in nutrition in Australia, with over 100 peer-reviewed publications. He has served on National Health and Medical Research Council working parties for reviews of Dietary Guidelines for Australia and Nutrient Reference Values, and has been a member of the Board of Food Standards Australia New Zealand and the Heart Foundation's Food and Nutrition Advisory Committee. He has also conducted consultancy projects with the NSW Department of Health to help develop nutrition standards and therapeutic diet specifications for adult hospital inpatients.

Website: http://peterwilliams1.weebly.com

www.ingramcontent.com/pod-product-compliance
Lightning Source LLC
Chambersburg PA
CBHW041517220426
43667CB00002B/20